Lead Sell Care
AS EASY AS 123

It's time to get back to basics!

Common Denominator of a Successful Business

JASON B. MONTANEZ

Lead, Sell, Care As Easy as 1,2,3

Book design by Inka Mathew, Green Ink Studio (greeninkstudio.com)

Acknowledgments

I would be remiss if I did not thank God for everything that I have, everything that I don't have, and all the great things that will happen in my life. I thank my parents for giving me a great upbringing and my mom for not only being my rock, but for being my editor–in-chief for this book. I thank my dad for instilling the positive way of thinking and showing me the power that the mind has on one's life. I thank my sons, Jordan & Jonavan for continuing to inspire me everyday to be a better father and person. I will always have your backs. Thank you to all of my mentors past and present that have had a positive influence on my life. You are all appreciated! To all the very good leaders and the very poor leaders that I have had the honor of working with. You have shown me what to do and what not to do, and it has worked. Lastly, but certainly not least, I would like to thank all those that I have led that have inspired me to write this book and have taken me to the top in every leadership position that I have ever had. You, the reader, will be guaranteed success if you continue to apply the simple principles and lessons found in the following pages. I am grateful for everyone and everything that I have experienced and will experience in my life. Thank You!

About the Author

For the past 15 years Jason B. Montanez has been leading, motivating, and inspiring people all across the United States. Whether it was on the football field, in a call center, in a retail store, or in a corporate office, Jason has helped others to realize their highest abilities in leadership, sales, and care.

After spending eleven years in Corporate America, Jason decided that his impact was not as great as he would like. In other words, his ability to influence people was somewhat limited to the people in his organization. Through his experiences and the experiences of others, Jason decided to start The Catapult Leadership Group to "Launch the Leader" in everyone through leadership, sales, and customer care. Why? Because Jason believes that everybody possesses leadership qualities and tendencies, but some need a GPS to guide them to their destination. Also, Jason firmly believes and has great conviction, that if one focuses on being a great leader, a great salesperson, and actually cares about himself and others, that success will be imminent professionally and personally.

Educationally, Jason holds two Bachelor's Degrees (Communication & Psychology) from the University at Buffalo, an M.B.A. with a concentration in Leadership from Tiffin University, and an Executive Leadership Certificate from Notre Dame University's Mendoza School of Business.

Born in Brooklyn, NY and raised in Spring Valley, NY, Jason now resides in Houston, TX.

Table of Contents

Table of Contents

Introduction

No, I have not been CEO of a Fortune 500 company, have not rubbed elbows with Bill Gates, Warren Buffet, or Mayor Bloomberg, and no, I am not currently a leading authority on leadership; yet! However, I am very passionate about leadership, sales, and care. I have led at the frontlines of a very successful Fortune 500 company that was the leader in its respective industry, and have touched the lives of many employees with whom I have served. In a nutshell, I have been successful in the various roles that I have held and have always been considered a leader amongst my subordinates, superiors, and peers. That being said, I am writing this book from a frontline employee perspective based on my experiences. Although theory has its place in teaching leadership, you will not see it anywhere in this book. What you will see are pragmatic ways to strengthen **L**eadership, **S**ales, and **C**are performance. The title of this book LSC as easy as 1,2,3 is an oxymoron in every sense of the word. In fact being a great **L**eader, a great **S**alesperson, and Providing **C**are has been and continues to be difficult in today's workforce. If it were easy, everybody would be doing it consistently at a very high level. It is my contention that if organizations spend most of their energy on these three facets at the frontline level (those that have everyday interactions with customers) not only will employee and customer retention be high, but they will be attractive to prospective customers and talented employees—resulting in true growth. So, grab yourself a beverage, get your reading glasses (if you need them), and let us become better **L**eaders, **S**alespeople, and Providers of **C**are. Enjoy!

Preface

You want to move the bottom-line? Lead the frontline!

Believe it or not, there are thoughts that are never heard, feelings that are never shown, and questions that are never answered from the most important people in every organization — the FRONT-LINE EMPLOYEE! Why? It's simple, they're never asked! An inclusive culture does not exist where their opinions are valued, or perhaps they fear retaliation for speaking against the status quo or offering solutions that are inconsistent with the current direction. In other words, apprehension exists because employees do not want to be labeled as the ones not drinking the Kool Aid. Constructive dissent from the frontline should not only be appreciated, but it should be required in today's workplace. Solutions can be found at any level of the organization that may perhaps be the next competitive advantage for the business.

One might ask why some organizations never see breakthrough results. Month after month, quarter after quarter, and year after year results remain stagnant or increase minimally; or even in some cases yield negative results. Why is this? Lack of Leadership at the frontlines! Frontline employees do not feel valued and employees are not empowered to lead. Furthermore, some frontline employees simply do not care. Where does all this come from? I thought you would never ask! It is the existant culture that fosters such lack luster performance. Have no fear, all this can be changed. It has been my experience that Leadership is the main catalyst in realizing breakthrough results. It has also been my experience that common sense is not too common in corporate America or business in general. Countless times I have sat in groups of so called "leaders" with Upper Management's intent to teach frontline managers how to lead. Often times, expensive outside sources were hired to serve as "leadership saviors". As I sat through these one or sometimes two-day theoretically based lectures, I thought to myself, "I know all of this. Much of what is regurgitated is common sense. This is déjà vu—Leadership 101." It was common sense to me; however, as I looked around and saw my peers having "Aha" moments, I knew there was a greater problem. These peers consisted of well tenured managers with over 15–20 years of so called Management experience. This couldn't be! For this reason, I decided to write this book to help others enhance their **L**eadership, **S**ales, & **C**are skills. I think any businessman or woman would agree that there are three fundamental keys to being successful in business; High level **L**eadership, High level **S**ales, & High level **C**are. The term High refers to transcending above the norm or whatever is acceptable for leadership, sales, and care within the given organization. Of course, every organization will have different measurements and ways to quantify what is or is not acceptable; however, if the norm is used as the baseline, success will result because transcending occurs. When I think of the word transcend, I think of going all out to maximize and realize one's full potential or making the impossible possible. My football coach used to utter the phrase "leave it all out on the field", in other words give it all you've got!

Nowadays, in this competitive and ever-changing business climate, consumers have options, this is why organizations must take care of (listen, reward, compensate, include) their internal customers (their employees) to ensure that they gain and retain external customers (grow). At the end of the day, the formula is simple; take care of your frontline employees + take care of your customers = Success.

One aspect that has been consistent throughout my professional career (over 15 years of **LSC** experience) is my focus on the frontline employee and frontline leadership. Why? Because these are the people representing the organization. These are the people that interact with customers and potential customers who will formulate an opinion of your brand that may never be able to be reconciled if they encounter a negative experience. These are the people that work long hours and that have to deal with the happy or unhappy customers based on policies/procedures that have been handed down to them. I was one of them! I know! Is the picture painted? Seems like a no brainer, right? One would be surprised with the decisions made in today's organizations whether they are policy or procedural in nature or just because "this is the way we do business." On the other hand, one would probably not be surprised because he or she is a customer of yours that has experienced the wrath of an outdated policy or procedure; food for thought? How many of you have asked the question, "Why are we doing things this particular way?" A response such as, "Because this is the way that it's always been done!", is not an acceptable one. Businesses that function this way and stick to procedures because it's just the way it's always been done will eventually become obsolete! How many of us have had the guts to question or tell a higher executive that what was experienced at the frontline was a thoughtless policy or procedure—not in a disrespectful manner, but in a thought provoking way. Is your organization receptive to ideas that they may not want to hear or that may challenge their ways of thinking? Critical thinking is exactly what it says it is; critical! Organizations must embrace, teach, and foster environments of critical thinking.

True leaders seek challenges and want to be challenged. They do not mind being questioned because it gives them a chance to see how well versed they are in their ability to influence. True leaders do not have a "do as I say" attitude just because I am the boss or at the top of some hierarchy. What kind of leaders do you have? What kind of leaders do you cultivate? Do you have managers or leaders in your organization? Managers adhere to directives handed down to them and ensure that policies and procedures are followed to a T. Leaders recognize potential issues, think innovatively, offer solutions, challenge the status quo, and provide direction when the organizational GPS seems to be malfunctioning. Leaders have the vision coupled with the energy and motivation necessary to influence change in people. That being said, organizations must select their leaders carefully. Let me clarify one point before I go on. Leaders lead people and Managers lead projects. This will be discussed further in detail under the Leadership section of the **LSC** model.

I have had the experience and pleasure of working in a Call Center environment as a frontline employee focusing on Caring, Leading customer service representatives, Leading retail sales representatives, and selling products and services to enterprise clientele. One constant in these various environments is that Sales has to Care, Care has to Sell, and Leaders are needed to Lead. With the Universal Model (where individuals are trained cross functionally and asked to do more) being more prevalent in today's business model, it is imperative for organizations to understand this to sustain themselves as a competitive force. The days of "That's not in my job description!" are gone and everyone, regardless of title, must Lead, Sell, and Care!

This book is more about application and bringing the real deal to organizations. Sure, knowledge and theory are good, but what good are they without application? What good is having potential if it is never realized? What good is having a gift and not sharing it with others? You know, one of my mentors introduced me to Yoda (formerly of the Star Wars) after he asked me, "Jason is your team of employees going to be the most productive team in the Call Center again this month?" I replied, "I am sure going to try!" He responded, "Jason, have you heard of Yoda?".... "Yes", I replied. He stated wisely, "Jason, you either Do or you Don't—there is no try!" That one encounter had such a profound impact on both my professional and personal growth that I cannot help but keep on doing what my passion is—Leading, Selling, and Caring. Ladies and gentlemen buckle your seatbelts on this journey as I give you the real deal on Leading, Selling, and Caring from the frontline. I promise to challenge your ways of thinking through insightful and self reflecting questions that will not only help you to grow professionally but personally as well. Moreover, whether you are Leading, Selling, or Caring, people desire a sincere genuineness with a smile when interacting. Furthermore, it is my goal to help the organizations that you work for transcend their results because your potential will have been maximized and realized. Open your minds, be free from worry, and focus on controlling only what you can control. Let my energy, passion, and motivation be evident through my pen. First stop on the transcending journey is Leadership.

Nowadays, in a world where there is much economic uncertainty, the one constant that has emerged and is of the utmost importance is the concept of having great leadership. Furthermore, competition is so tough and the playing field is so even that the main difference will be the leadership that is in place at organizations. Leadership is a phenomenon that I found very interesting since my early days as captain of my High School football team. I did not know it at the time, but looking back I was not elected team captain because of talent (believe it or not I wasn't the biggest, strongest, or fastest) but because I displayed the discipline, the heart, the courage, and the unwavering commitment to excellence that was not common amongst teenagers. Great Leaders are not common. When you think of a great Leader, who stands out in your mind? I know when I do it is a group that looks like this: Dr. Martin Luther King Jr., George Washington, Abraham Lincoln, Adolf Hitler, Sadaam Hussein, Mao Zedong, Mahatma Ghandi…etc., the list goes on and on. Ponder this: Every one of the aforementioned leaders stood for something, good or bad that he was passionate about and had the ability to bring his vision to reality by convincing people to follow irrespective of whether it was derived from inspiration or intimidation. I emphasize the word people. There are different types of people. A true leader has the ability to visualize and tap into the emotions of people from all walks of life to follow his or her lead. That being said, does one lead the same way with everyone? How does one lead or obtain the leadership skill to influence or inspire others to follow? An effective leader needs to have the ability to Adapt and Associate also known as A&A. There is a prerequisite to A&A and that is the ability to Listen. A wise man once told me, "Jason you have two ears and one mouth. You need to listen two times more than you speak." As one listens, it invokes thought and helps formulate strategies on how to adapt and associate effectively. In a nutshell, listening results in engagement and engagement by all in the organization is a fundamental key to success.

A&A

As I stated previously, there is no one "right way" to lead. Through adaptation a leader will know which skill set to use when warranted. For example, as a customer service manager I had the opportunity to serve employees (people) from different parts of the United States. Furthermore, when I relocated from New York to Wilmington, NC to Albuquerque, NM, and finally to Houston, TX, I had to adapt to the culture and a new way of life that was very different in each locale. I had to be receptive to what my followers had to say in order for me to utilize my leadership skills. In other words, I had to be a chameleon and become one of them. I had to show that I understood them. I had to reinvent myself. I had to adapt while being flexible and agile. By no means did I lose my identity or give up my values, but I had to borrow a tool from my followers in order to assemble a solid following.

Association is probably the most important emotion in LSC. The ability to associate is profound in the sense that you can feel what others feel; sometimes before they utter a word. Those who possess a high ability to associate with others will have a greater ability to Lead, Sell, & Care.

REAL EXPERIENCE: I had an employee by the name of Amy. She was known as a "problem" employee (one who gave managers a hard time) before she came on my team. As a matter of fact, no one wanted Amy on their team so it was decided to put her on my team because they thought I could handle her personality. The first thing that I did with Amy was to meet with her about nothing work related just to talk and to see what her goals and aspirations were in life. Amy was non-receptive to this meeting because as she told me, "her previous experiences with management were phony and she had no trust in management because of giving her false hopes over promotion." Immediately, I realized what made Amy tick was the ability to get promoted. As the meeting progressed, Amy revealed her passion for graphic design and creating websites. Amy revealed that her ideal job would be to create websites and online tools to help employees with their jobs. From that point on I dubbed Amy as my Reward and Recognition subject matter expert (SME). Amy would be charged with developing contests that reward and recognize fellow employees on the team which simultaneously honed in on her graphic design talent. Boy did Amy do a wonderful job! We had contests that were fun and that increased our productivity with much of the responsibility going to Amy. My boss came up to me and said, "Jason it seems like Amy has turned over a new leaf; what did you do?" I replied, "I did what no others did, I listened!" The long and short of it is that Amy did such a great job for me that once an opportunity presented itself to work on the company intranet, she interviewed and utilized all the work she did for my team and got the job! The moral of the story is that every organization has an Amy or maybe a bunch of Amys that have great talent and potential but are not being heard. All it takes is for one manager to fail them and their whole perspective of leadership is misconstrued. This faux-pas ultimately affects the organization because a full salary is being paid to someone who is only offering 50% of his/her talent. You do the math. Does that make any sense?

Adapting & Associating is no walk in the park by any means. What does a 60 year old baby boomer have in common with a Generation Z 21 year old? Besides breathing the same air—absolutely nothing! Between the two generations there are different ideologies, motivators, behaviors, attitudes, expectations, and habits. One difference that really stands out to me is that a baby boomer employee will ask the question, "What time do I work?" and a Generation Z employee will ask, "What time do I get off?" That's not the half. There are 4 generations working together in today's workforce and a leader must manage each employee with great versatility. Challenging? Very much so. So what's the challenge? The challenge is to bring people together that not only have diverse cultural backgrounds and values, but that bring their own distinct differences with regards to views of the world.

I am a firm believer that one's employees do not have to be friends or necessarily get along in the workplace. Sure this would be ideal and utopia as we know it, however, if a leader finds common ground and directs the team towards a common goal with extrinsic motivators—the team will succeed. Case in point: In High School my football team boasted the best record in school history and 16 years later it still stands (11-1). Not all of our teammates liked each other. As a matter of fact, there were individual clicks that made up the team and fights ensued when tempers flared. But at the end of the day, we had a leader that cared about us, always pointed us in the same direction, and was unwavering in that direction to get us to Syracuse to win the State Championship. In order to do so we had to respect one another. We did not have to like each other or hang out together after practice or a game. We were a family. This is the same in business. Do you like everyone in your family? Is there anyone in your family that you cannot stand? Exactly my point! Furthermore, through A&A a leader must leverage key ingredients by getting to know his subordinates on a personal level. How? Sit down and ask what makes them tick? What motivates them? What irritates them? What are their goals/aspirations in life? Oh here's a good one... What is their perception of you as a leader or as a person in general? Is it in line with who you want them to believe you are or are they way off? What are their day to day challenges? What can you do to lessen the burden on them? A&A promotes and builds discipleship. A wise, old man once told me," Jason, people do not care about what you know until they know that you care." Leaders, go Adapt & Associate!

WHAT MAKES
A CATAPULT LEADER?

There are distinct characteristics or a specific make-up that craft Catapult leaders. I use the word Catapult because they have the ability to launch the leader within people. Catapult Leaders are cut from a different type of cloth, but have no fear; the Catapult Leader cloth can be woven into any style with the proper will and attitude to make an impact. Now, Catapult Leaders are different than Leaders. Let's first make it crystal clear: it is necessary to have Managers, Leaders, and Catapult Leaders to catapult and sustain breakthrough results in all organizations. Just like all championship teams need role players; so do organizations. It has been my experience that the following identifies each role:

MANAGERS: oversee projects, are good with managing timelines, making deadlines, and running reports for upper management. Furthermore, managers may have subordinates but they have no desire to excel or to be the very best. Managers keep the boat afloat and do just enough to ensure that their teams are not tanking it. In other words, they are satisfied with mediocrity. Building relationships or the development of others is not a top priority. Managers have a do as I say because I am the manager attitude. Additionally, subordinates may or may not follow a manager based on his or her title. Subsequent discussions will focus on how subordinates really have the option to follow or not to follow.

LEADERS: are versatile. They can Adapt & Associate (A&A) to any generation, background, race, ethnicity, gender, sexual preference, or way of thinking. Leaders care about building relationships and developing others. Leaders want to make subordinates, superiors, and peers better by challenging them. They create a participatory culture and delegate effectively. Leaders have a "can do" attitude because they firmly believe there is nothing that one cannot do. Critical thinking and solution-based thinking are promoted and encouraged. Leaders emerge at any level of an organization. The following is a list of additional characteristics of great leaders:

self reflecting	charismatic
associate with winners	disassociate with losers
have a high ethical standard	act with Integrity
listener	think critically
intellectual	disciplined
supportive	are wise
courageous	display good judgment
objective	inspiring
encouraging	stand up against what is wrong
understanding	patient
have a Sense of Urgency	coach by example
offer solutions	control what they can control
Keep it Real!	

CATAPULT LEADERS: do everything that leaders do and possess all of the aforementioned qualities. The one significant difference between a Leader and a Catapult Leader is the fact that a Catapult Leader can do it over, and over, and over again at a very high level, with different teams (people) in a short period of time and master change. A Leader excels most of the time, but a Catapult leader excels all of the time. Catapult leaders have the ability to create synergy that transcends above the possible and smashes the impossible. People follow Catapult leaders sometimes just because of who they are and their legacy. Catapult leaders catapult vision into reality. The effect of the catapult leader lives on long after they are gone. The Catapult leader is unwavering in his conviction and executes by holding himself and others accountable. In your view, who are some Catapult leaders? Have you ever experienced a Catapult leader? What kind of impact did they have on who you are today? Are you a Catapult leader?

In my opinion, a more recent Catapult leader is President Barack Obama. Let's throw out the fact that he was the first African American President of the United States of America. Let's throw out the fact that he represents the Democratic political party. Let's throw out everything he stands for politically whether or not you are in agreement with his political views. Let's focus on his 2008 campaign slogan "Yes we can!". Let's just focus on those three words for a moment. President Obama listened to the people of the United States and capitalized on the emotions of the people. The United States was in financial turmoil in so many ways and hope seemed nonexistent. "Yes we can" gave hope to so many Americans despite political party, race, ethnicity, gender, or sexual preference. The slogan "Yes we can" is diverse in its own right in the sense that everyone can finish the sentence and customize it to themselves. These 3 words "Yes we can" are very aggressive and powerful. They shine rays of togetherness, unity, participation, coupled with a "can do" attitude. Furthermore, all the characteristics of a Catapult leader are unwavering in nature. The ability to unite people from different walks of life and perspectives in order to focus on a common goal is what leadership is all about. It is turning a vision into a reality. The legacy developed by Catapult leaders lives on when the leader moves on.

THE THREE- LEGGED STOOL OF LEADERSHIP

In order to be an effective leader three things (legs) must be present. I call it the three-legged stool of leadership. I use the three-legged stool analogy because if any of these critical legs are missing a leader will fall flat on his rear end! The three legs are Ability, Awareness, & Will. An effective leader must have all three to be successful. How successful he or she is depends on the effort placed to develop these three critical skill sets. If all three legs are strong, the leader will sit upon a solid leadership foundation without worry. If any of the legs are weak and the leader does not pay attention or do anything to strengthen that leg, he or she will take a mean and sometimes embarrassing fall if others are watching.

ABILITY

I firmly believe that everyone can gain the ability to be a successful and effective leader. Some have an innate ability to lead and others can definitely work towards their leadership ability. Being an effective leader is an ongoing process as business is ever changing and so are people. Being a leader is not easy and gaining the skill set to lead is not either. Leadership is demanding and it needs continuous work. Styles of leadership vary and some may argue that no one style is the "right way" to lead. I believe the concept of serving and giving are the most effective. It is very important to not put all your leadership eggs in one basket. What I mean by this is to not invest all of your time in focusing on one style because a great leader's style will be eclectic and he/she will know which style to use in any given situation.

That being said, ability plays a very important role and is one of the three-legged pillars because if the leader does not have the skill set to lead, he or she cannot be an effective leader. If the leader does not have a powerful enough ability to influence behavior then his/her effectiveness is minimized. The ability to make hard decisions or unpopular decisions is also key. If the leader is more concerned with popularity or making decisions that will get him/her accepted, the ability leg will be weak. Charisma also has its place under the realm of ability. It is the nails, screws, and glue that keep the three-legged leadership stool together. While I have witnessed leaders become successful without an ounce of charisma, it just makes it easier for individuals to follow someone that has a nice appearance, a sense of humor, and is down to earth. In other words, someone who has some swagger!

AWARENESS

Are you present both physically and mentally? Seriously, are you really? Do you realize how people perceive you? Are you aware of the decisions that you make and the impact that they have not only on yourself but on others?

These are some key questions that leaders have to ask themselves to be truly effective. Awareness is probably the most important of the three legs. Are you receptive to constructive feedback? Do you seek feedback? If you get feedback are you listening and not just hearing? Being aware also has to deal with always keeping one's ear to the ground to ensure that the best possible decisions are being made. Often times, leaders depend on others to be their awareness and somewhere along the line the reality gets blurred and decisions are made that do not benefit the real organization but the perceived organization. What I mean by this is that if you are not aware and disengaged from the business, decisions will be made based on the way you think things are as opposed to the way things really are. If one believes in heavy delegation and empowerment, it is critical that a high level of communication and transparency exists in order to be fully aware.

WILL

Skill vs. Will has been a debate for some time when referring to one's ability to get a job done or complete a task. Some argue that it can either be the skill level or the Will level of the individual. Well, in the three-legged stool of leadership model, both ability (Skill) and Will must exist to be an effective leader. Having the will to lead is very important. It takes a great deal of commitment and sacrifice to lead. Believe it or not, I have seen people promoted to leadership positions that have no desire to lead. Later in this book I will address the fact that people cannot be forced to lead. Are you willing to take none of the credit when the team succeeds and all of the credit when the team fails? One's will to lead has to be genuine! It is very easy to see when the Will and the commitment are not real. It will be very hard to influence behavior and get people to follow your lead if you yourself are not authentic. As stated earlier, a leader must be unwavering in his commitment and must weather the storm so to speak when adversity or challenges arise, and they will! You must have the Will! Do you have the Will to be an effective leader?

To be an effective leader one must ensure that the three legs on the stool are strong by continuously engaging in activities to strengthen them. Some have the Ability and Awareness but struggle with the Will. In other words, they are not fully committed. Others are committed and able but just not aware. This results in bad decision making. Some can be committed and aware but just do not have the influence ability to be an effective leader. Perhaps it is a lack of charisma or failure to articulate the vision clearly. In a nutshell, all three legs must be in excellent shape to support the weight of being a leader. If not, the leader will fall flat on his derrière!

ATTITUDE

"Yes we can" is an attitude; a way of life. As a proud parent of two boys, it is in their best interest that I have a "Yes we can" or a "can do" attitude. It has been my experience that leadership has to do with attitude. Attitude is contagious and infectious irrespective of whether it is positive or negative in nature. What else is contagious? Energy, approach, passion, and discipline are just a few. Leadership, Sales, & Care have to do with attitude. As a matter of fact, life in general has to do with attitude. How do you see life? Is the cup half full or is the cup half empty? One day I was in a coaching session with one of my employees and we were talking about attitudes and how your attitude/demeanor is very hard to mask because that is just who you are. That employee was twenty-seven years older than me and he taught me 3 letters that he lived by, "CYA". I asked him what that stood for and he replied, "Choose Your Attitude." When we talk about leaders controlling what they can control, attitude is at the crest of the control wave. In life, there will be circumstances that we can and cannot control. It makes absolutely no sense to have feelings or changes in attitude based on things that we cannot control. However, guess what? We're human! Sometimes we may fall to the trough of the control wave and worry, focus, or try to change things that we have absolutely no control over. This is where leadership comes in. Not everyone has the ability to decipher what is above the water line or below the water line; what is above the surface or below the surface; what can be controlled or what cannot be controlled. It is the leader's duty to recognize and help develop this ability in others to determine what can and cannot be controlled. Remember, one of the characteristics of a leader is the ability to control what is controllable. A prayer that my mom gave me early on in life best fits this discussion. It is called the Serenity prayer and it is as follows: "God, grant me the serenity to accept the things that I cannot change, the courage to change the things I can, and the wisdom to know the difference." So, ladies and gentlemen, CYA!

After having that coaching session with my employee, I decided to facilitate a discussion about attitude at my weekly staff meeting. Visualize this! Have you ever known someone, had a peer, a boss, or a subordinate whose attitude seemed to vacillate no matter what transpired? Or at a moment's notice something changed their entire day from a smile to a frown as if the sun was not shining brightly enough! By the way, is that something that we can control? Well, I have had employees that allow issues like the weather or traffic to just jack-up their whole attitude. Why? Because we are human and humans struggle with deciphering between what they can and cannot control, consequently affecting their attitudes and productivity. Is the picture painted?

TRUE STORY: So, here I am in my staff meeting facilitating a discussion about attitudes and how it impacts sales performance and the discussion is going very well amongst the team members with complete and active participation. After about ten minutes of setting the discussion up for the acronym that my employee shared with me earlier in the week, I state with great enthusiasm and passion, "Team all we have to do every day is CYA!"

Suddenly, the same employee that we just described says, "what, Cover Your Ass?" As I stood there in amazement, I realized that attitude is more important than ever because it is derived from the way one feels, to the way one thinks, which eventually dictates the way one behaves. Leaders must promote positive, energetic, and passionate attitudes and obliterate all negative attitudes. As I stated earlier, attitudes are contagious regardless of whether they are positive or negative in nature. Leaders shape thoughts that promote and reinforce positive, optimistic, and "can do" attitudes. Additionally, catapult leaders are unwavering (black or white) with regards to their attitude. Attitude can be good or bad, right or wrong, do or do not, and win or lose. There is no middle ground.

TURN THE CHANNEL TO A&E

No, we are not going to watch shows like Pawn Stars, Storage Wars, Duck Dynasty, The First 48 or any other popular shows via cable TV, however, we are going to use the example of the remote control because we all have the ability to control certain aspects of our lives and we should focus on these things to be better people in society. Like the TV remote, we have it in our hands! Two things that people have absolute control over are their attitude and their effort. Thus, we must channel our Attitude & Effort also known as channeling our A&E. This is a lot easier said than done. Most people do not know how to channel their attitude and effort. That is where the leader comes in and provides assistance. Before leading people to channel their A&E, it is imperative that the leader gets to know his followers on a personal level and they themselves have the ability to channel their attitude and effort. In order for a follower to open up on a personal level, trust must be established. So, how does one establish trust? First of all, be a model—lead by example (do not require of others what you would not require of yourself), do what you said you were going to do (keep your word), show a genuine sense of care (your vulnerability) and others will do likewise. Naturally, anyone who has ever been around me knows that I am always happy. You will often find me singing, laughing, or smiling. People often ask me if I am happy and energetic all the time. The answer is no! What I can say is that I have mastered the way to use my internal remote (my mind) to channel my Attitude & Effort. I learned very quickly from a subordinate that Attitude & Effort are not the only channels on our remote controls. When I presented this concept to one of my teams one of my employees said, "You can also control your Excitement, Energy, Engagement, and Enthusiasm." She was obviously engaged ☺. So, whatever it is that you need to control make sure you use your remote to control your A&E. Personally, I have programmed my remote to think inside the box.

THINK INSIDE THE BOX!

I have often heard the term, "You've got to think outside the box" when groups want to innovate and brainstorm ways to be effective. I agree with this to a certain extent, however, I believe that it is more effective to think inside the box. The box that I am referring to is the box of control that everyone possesses. This box can be found between the ears of any living, breathing, and pulsating human. Often times, people stunt their growth and productivity by allowing circumstances that are outside of their realm of control to affect them personally, which in turn has a harmful impact on their decision making process. I firmly believe that the main difference between a successful person and an unsuccessful person is his/her thought process. Focus your energy on what is inside the box and feed it positivity, optimism, and hope. Do not focus on the issues that you have absolutely no control over.

Inside this box is also home to one's values, morals, and character. Everyone must ask himself, "What do I value?" The response will serve to formulate morals (what is right & wrong). This in turn, will develop character (how one regularly acts and the decisions that one habitually makes). Sure, there can be outside influences that impact one's behavior, however, if we pay close attention to what is inside the box, the result will be ethical and moral decision making and an indisputable positive character.

That which the leader values, directly impacts the direction of his decision making. For example, a company that values customer loyalty will be more inclined to make policies that are conducive to the customer's preferences. On the contrary, a company that has tunnel vision and only values profitability/revenues and not the customer, will make less customer friendly policies.

The leader's style is directly impacted by his values. A leader that values family and holds a high regard for work/life balance will lead differently than one who holds great value to moving up the corporate ladder as swiftly as possible. As you can imagine, the experience from either one of their subordinates will be on opposite ends of the spectrum. This is the reason why it is very important in leadership and thinking inside the box to foster the ability to be self aware and self-reflective. A more systematic and better decision making process will result if one has the ability to look in the mirror and have the courage to be honest. Being aware of how one's actions and decisions impact others is one of the key principles of leadership as discussed in the three-legged stool. Will your actions or decisions result in apathy or increased energy?

TURNING APATHETIC TO ENERGETIC

Are your employees showing no interest, no energy, no sense of urgency, no enthusiasm, and are they content with just being present? As a leader you will have to deal with those that are content with mediocrity. This apathy that we are referring to can be just the social make-up of the employee or it can be a result of some outside influence which may be you! So the question is: how does one convert a worker who has absolutely zero motivation to be the best, into one who cares not only about his personal success, but the success of the team or organization as a whole? All people want to be successful. All people want the best for themselves. All people want to feel fulfilled. It is your duty as the leader to bring it out. You see, some people have no motivation because they have never been motivated or inspired! Maybe they don't know how to motivate themselves. Maybe they have only heard about success and never realized success. Maybe they have had negative experiences and they have put up a psychological block that does not allow them to succeed. So, how do you help them to reach their potential?

Thinking is very critical! How one thinks and perceives oneself and the world is essential to the success of your organization. I have always taken the stance with my teams that I was making each and every one of them a better citizen for the community and in turn they would be better employees for me. I am a firm believer that in business if you cultivate better people you will reap the rewards. I did this by getting to know them and understanding what made them tick. Whenever, I would hear negativity come out of their mouths, I would rebuke it with positive reinforcement demonstrating how that negative thinking affects what is important to them, again, having nothing to do with work. It has worked.

REAL TALK: Ricardo, was an employee of mine that had great technical knowledge, probably the best on my team, however, he had this attitude that everyone had it out for him and probably gave his best about fifty percent of the time. Furthermore, there was a conspiracy shadow that always followed him no matter where he went that did not allow him to succeed. In his own words, "Someone's out to get me, I just can't win!" So, one day Ricardo and I were in a coaching session where he failed a quality assurance call and that same conspiracy theory attitude exuded from him. What I did notice was that there were pictures of his family tacked throughout his cubicle and that he and his wife were both working to make ends meet. I shifted the conversation away from work and asked Ricardo who took care of his children while he and his wife were at work. He looked at me with this baffled look and said, "I have a really good baby sitter" I then asked, "What makes her really good?" He replied, "She's reliable, she has great knowledge of how to care for children, and she's a family woman. Jason, what does this have to do with this call?" I replied, "Ricardo, just like your baby sitter, I think you are reliable, have great knowledge of what you are doing, and are a family man. Am I correct?" He replied, "Yes." I went on to say, "I'm going to ask you a question that I don't want you to answer but just give some thought to it. What if I told you that your baby sitter has this attitude that someone's always out to get her and she's taking care of your children for only four hours of the day and not for the full eight hours? How would you feel? What would you do?" I immediately ended the coaching session. Ricardo came in the next day with a renewed attitude and never looked back. The transformation was amazing. Ricardo was now energized and no apathy was left in his bones. Just last week I received a message from Ricardo and his email signature read that he was now in a leadership role.

There is a certain psychology that one must have to be the best at what one wants to become. It is an unrelenting attitude that rebukes negativity/pessimism and epitomizes positivity/optimism. The great aspect about it is that this cognition is free, and as the leader you must grasp it and disseminate it! Sell it! People like free!

CATAPULT LEADERS ARE WISE, NOT SMART!

I once heard the saying, "A smart person learns from his or her mistakes, but a wise person learns from the mistakes of others." In other words, someone who is wise does not necessarily have to go through a situation to learn how to manage it, prevent it, or be good at it. This brings up another provocative question. Does one have to be older in chronological age, more tenured in a job, or have more "life experience" to be wise? What causes one to be wise and have the attitude that learning through observation, listening astutely, and learning from the indiscretions of others is key to catapulting leadership not only within themselves, but in leading others?

In leadership, it is best to be wise in creating and nurturing relationships with those you will be guiding, those who are your colleagues, and those in a supervisory capacity. If the "Golden Rule" does not work for you, then observe another leader that does very well in communicating with others. Understand that in order for communication to be effective, there has to be a message sent, a message received, and a message sent back; similar to a boomerang. Simply making a statement, sending an email, sending out a mass text message, or writing a message on a communication board are not considered effective ways of communicating. Focusing on and being wise about communication is key. Unfortunately, just being smart about communication will not suffice. Going about communication the wrong way initially can be detrimental in building a long-term relationship. Surely it can be said that tough lessons have been learned from instances of miscommunicating. However, people do not have short memories in Corporate America or in life in general. Have you ever heard of the saying, "I can forgive, but I will never forget?" When I played football and our quarterback threw an interception the head coach would walk over to him, pat him on the back and say, "You got to have a short memory kid, shrug it off and get back out there on the next series." Unfortunately, it is not that easy in the workplace. Often times, if the initial communication is not received properly, the relationship takes a very long time to be repaired to the level that it could have been if the initial communication had been transmitted effectively. Furthermore, sometimes the relationship never gets repaired and the full potential of the employee is never realized. By the way, this is no bueno! (not good).

Let me tell you a story about Jeramy. When I was an Assistant Manager, Jeramy was my manager or the one that I reported to. Jeramy was 27 years older than me, as a matter of fact, he had children my age and older than me. Jeramy worked for many years, had a business which he sold for good money, and managed a Big Box retailer with over one hundred employees reporting to him. As an outsider looking in would you say Jeramy has good work experience, has tenure, and is very experienced in life? I would agree. There was one thing missing though. Jeramy was smart but not wise. During much of the time with Jeramy, I had to put out fires and de-escalate situations between him and employees because of the way that he chose to communicate. It was usually with a "do as I say" attitude because I am the boss. Jeramy was also coercive in nature. Coercion does not work in today's workforce. Employee sabotage will be addressed later in this chapter. Jeramy would declare, "If you do not do this, then you will be written up!" Jeramy was a nice guy, but his communication was off. This caused the team of representatives to not give their all, which caused the location as a whole to suffer. The situation deteriorated so rapidly that Human Resources was summoned to mediate. Once Human Resources intervened and interviewed Jeramy as well as the employees, Jeramy did change his tune. However, remember as stated earlier, there are no short memories in corporate America. Yes, there was less conflict between Jeramy and the employees, but the damage had already been done. The relationship was irreparable and the employees only gave minimal productivity due to the barrier already in place as a result of their previous experiences. Could this have been avoided? I am pretty sure that Jeramy must have observed a leader in the course of his lifetime and work experience where he could have been wise about his communication style, right? Jeramy was smart because he learned from his mistakes. Once Human Resources came in to mediate, he changed his communication style, but it was too late. Jeramy was ultimately terminated in an organizational downsize because he was considered a bottom performer. There is no doubt in my mind that if the initial communication was effective and Jeramy was wise and not smart, he would be employed to this day.

COMPLIANCE-BASED VS. VALUES-BASED LEADERSHIP

What is the driving force or motivation behind your leadership and decision making? What kinds of messages are you giving your employees? It is critical for one to ask oneself these questions in order to truly understand whether or not one is being an effective leader.

The compliance-based approach to leadership consists of fear or punishment from an external governor. Let me be clear that the external entity does not necessarily mean outside the organization but can be inter organizational but outside of the workgroup. An example of this would be having a sales team with the human resources team being the external entity. Both teams work for the same organization, however, the human resources team serves as the external team that enforces compliance issues. When leaders make decisions from the compliance-based approach, it is solely dependent on outside influences regarding why the decision is being made. To illustrate this idea, I will use an example of the JM trucking company assisting their drivers to be cognizant of their driving speed. The fleet manager conducts a meeting with his/her employees and says,

We must drive the speed limit because we cannot have a reputation with the police that we are poor drivers. We cannot afford anymore tickets as it is having a bad impact on our bottom-line. This has got to stop. Finance has set goals for us to be in-line with our company's priorities. Any more tickets and we will be forced to pass the cost through to your paychecks.

The same fleet manager conducts a meeting, but this time with a values based approach. The Leader says:

Team, an opportunity for improvement exists for us to watch our speed limit. At JM trucking one of our core values is ensuring your safety and the safety of others while on the road. It is important for us to be good corporate citizens and it is our responsibility to not only protect ourselves but others while operating our company vehicles. In the event that behaviors are not consistent with our core values pertaining to safety, specifically speeding, we will ask for you to absorb the costs associated with your actions. Thank you for your attention to this matter and living the JM trucking values.

What is the difference between these two approaches? In the compliance-based approach we see that the importance of the leadership revolves around being compliant with the speed limit (external factor), how the company is perceived (external), and metrics that finance has defined as compliant (external). In the values-based approach the leader talks to the importance of safety and acting responsibly because that is the JM trucking way (values). The company's core values are emphasized and the bottom-line is never mentioned. There is more concern towards living up to our internal standards (values) as opposed to external standards and a sense of accountability to those standards. Fear or punishment is not mentioned.

So, which is better? One can argue that at the end of the day either approach will yield a behavior change and I agree with that to an extent. What I do not believe is that the compliance-based approach to leadership is as effective as the values-based approach. I believe it is far more powerful and empowering to lead from a values-based approach. It teaches and develops your employees to make decisions from a values perspective rather than making decisions just to be compliant. I also believe that when decisions are made from within and from your heart so to speak, more energy and accountability results in better performance. In the JM trucking example, the drivers understanding from a values perspective promotes behavioral change from a value perspective resulting in genuine care about the company's direction. This can translate into better customer service, employee retention, a better sense of the employee adding value to the organization, and a feeling of rewarding work. The important detail is that organizations must recognize, reward, motivate, and train employees to do the right thing because it is the right thing to do based on the internal values, not because an external influence deems the behavior compliant.

THE DIFFERENCE

I have had the opportunity to work with good leaders and bad leaders. Primarily, let me disclose that the bad leaders were not bad people, just their leadership style was poor; for they were worried about being promoted and promoting their own agenda. Their rule was sovereign and an inclusive environment did not exist. Furthermore, it was clearly made known that they were the captains of the ship and the others in the group were just crew members that were to follow the direction of the leader. If one disagreed with the direction of the ship and voiced it, that individual would be labeled "the one not on board". The advantage in having been associated with bad leaders is that one learns instantly what not to do. If you felt a particular way because of the manner in which you were treated by your leader, the probability that others have or felt the same sentiment is very high. So, there is no need to be a rocket scientist and research what methodologies work and will not work;

all you have to do is observe and experience. It is a no brainer that the good leaders will get the most buy-in and effort out of their followers than a bad leader. As a matter of fact, catapult leaders coach and develop their followers to be leaders creating a culture of discipleship. Catapult leaders earn respect through admiration not fear. In John C. Maxwell's 360 degree Leader, he says that an effective leader commands and does not demand respect. I agree wholeheartedly. When one commands respect, the business continues to run at a high level even when the leader is not present. The psychology of the followers is that we cannot let our leader down at any cost because we know he/she cares about us.

One of my most challenging experiences occurred when I was selected to open a brand new retail location in an underpenetrated area. During the first five months, the location was producing great results which gave me great recognition. We had the best Grand Opening of any store in our Region and the store was performing better than stores that had been open for years. My name and my boss' name were shining in lights as sales drivers. Furthermore, the location was fully staffed and employees were happy and proud to be part of this new over-indexing location. What was yet to come was probably the worst experience of my professional career. I was unaware of the fact that my boss had advised three of my employees that they could move closer to home once they helped to open the new location. Once my boss reneged on his offer, those three employees completely shut down and there was nothing I could do to get them to give the best effort that they once gave because they felt they had been deceived. As a leader, once you lie and compromise trust with your followers, it will be very hard to turn them around. As a result, those three employees had mentally checked out. It cannot get any worse than this, right? WRONG! My assistant manager subsequently handed in her two-week notice of resignation. Ok, I can make it through this – I am a leader! The employees are talking amongst themselves and telling stories about how the District Manager lied to them and others are planning to jump ship as well. Oh no, how am I going to get my team back? Here we go again! An additional employee resigns to be part of a multi level marketing business and another is allowed to go to a store closer to home. Now everyone wants to go to another store and not go through the growing pains of opening a new location. All the while, sales are suffering, I am severely understaffed, I am working 12 hour shifts 6 days a week, and I am getting calls from my boss requesting greater performance. I remember vividly one of the conversations with my boss. He calls and says, "Jason, I need you to perform better". I responded, "Boss you got me playing the game with only seven people on the field when there are supposed to be eleven! How can you expect me to perform at the level that I was performing when you told people that you would move them and you didn't move them and when I come to you about filling my open positions, you are telling me to wait." My boss replies, "Jason, that's not going to fly, you are going to have to find a way to make it happen." At this point, for the first time in my career, I was ready to quit. I had a boss that was non receptive, wanted all the recognition for himself, was around and supportive when things were going well, but acted like he did not know me and was not part of the problem when performance declined. How can this type of leader be categorized—good or bad? I learned from this leader what not to do and I made a commitment to myself: NEVER make a subordinate feel this way. Furthermore, this faux pas was my entire fault! In retrospect, a catapult leader would have stood up, started jumping on his/her boss's desk for help, and if help did not arrive, a meeting with the boss' boss would have been scheduled. Where I went wrong was thinking that by going over my boss' head I would have been seen as a snitch or not cool. In the end, I had more loyalty to my boss than he had for me. I did not go above his head because I didn't want him to look bad. At the end of the day, I was the one to look bad and received a "developing" on my yearly appraisal because of my performance for the first-half of the year. Leaders take ownership, responsibility, and don't make excuses! I had to take this on the chin, but I learned.

SAY HELLO TO THE BAD GUY

To be an effective leader one must be strong willed, do what is right, and be willing to be sometimes labeled as the bad guy. There have been many times where employees have been upset with me because I made a decision that was not in-line with their way of thinking or what they wanted. For a while, I was labeled the bad guy because I did not give them what they wanted. Leaders get paid to make tough and unpopular decisions. This is probably the most challenging part of leadership because it is our humanistic intuition and according to Maslow's hierarchy of needs, it is a necessity to want to be needed, liked, loved, & wanted.

I have lived by this principle when making difficult decisions. **L**eadership, by acting with **I**ntegrity, being **F**air, thinking **E**thically, and always doing what's

Right (LIFER). If anyone gets upset with you when using these five principles in your decision making, it is well worth being labeled the bad guy. The biggest mistake in leadership is not making the right decision because you are afraid that you will be labeled the "bad guy." It is very easy to sweep things under the rug or cover up the flashing lights. Those that are labeled "the bad guys" make tough decisions, have the courage to tackle problems head on at the root, and care more about long-term success as opposed to short-term relief. In a nutshell, "the bad guy" is the one that really cares about the success of the organization. Let's make a clear distinction. The term "bad guy" refers to tough decisions that have to be made that are not the easiest, most popular, and most convenient courses of action to take. Furthermore, being a "bad guy" for no apparent reason and making dumb decisions just because you have the ability to do so is not being a "bad guy" it's being a "dumb guy." Self reflect: Are you a "bad guy" or a "dumb guy?"

I have been labeled the "bad guy" before. As a matter of fact, I've been labeled the "bad guy" many times. But here's the point! That "bad guy" title was temporary and not long-lasting. Once the team realized that the decisions that I was making were in the best interest of the team, I was "the respected guy", "the fair guy", "the consistent guy", and "the guy who really cares". When I played Linebacker in college, my defensive coordinator would always ride me and scold me when I made a mistake or missed an assignment on the field. Well, one day after practice, I had really messed up and I had my head down walking into the locker room and he said, "Jason, I yell at you and I'm hard on you because I know what kind of player you are and can become. Don't be worried about me yelling at you, be more worried about it if I ever stop. Then you'll know I have given up and I no longer Care."

TRUE STORY: Patrick, was a decent performer, was a likeable guy, and was a single father. There were times where he was outspoken in team meetings against changes that were being implemented from upper management, but I would not categorize him as a problem employee. There was however, a serious issue. Patrick was consistently late to work and his peers observed this. Often times, employees see things and take mental notes as a safeguard in the event that they themselves are ever in a similar situation. I had gone through the Verbal Warning, Written Warning, and Final Written Warning levels of corrective action and Patrick did not care enough to come to work on time. I offered Patrick company benefits to assist with his tardiness and probed to see if there were any underlying causes that factored into his lateness. Patrick said there were none. All the while, his peers were observing and anticipating what I as the Leader was going to do. I had a decision to make. Was I going to sweep it under the rug and let Patrick keep on coming to work late? I mean, he is well liked by his peers, he does a decent job, and he's not a problem employee. Or, do I terminate Patrick knowing he's a single father? Surely, my team would think I'm a "bad guy" if I push to terminate Patrick because it would seem that I have no heart. But, if I don't terminate Patrick for his tardiness and don't hold him accountable, I risk losing my whole team and they would no longer take me seriously. How can I coach others to be on time for work if they see that I do not hold the biggest offender accountable? Will this have a domino effect on other facets of the job? Sure it will. People respect accountability! What would you do? I will tell you what I did. I terminated Patrick and was labeled "the bad guy" for about two weeks. My decision was reaffirmed when no one else seemed to have an issue coming to work on time and my team performed at a high level for months afterwards because they knew there was an accountability measure. I could have ignored the issue at hand and taken the easy way out but I sacrificed the perception others had of me by using the LIFER principle. David Cottrell says it best in his book Monday Morning Leadership, "Ignoring issues puts your own integrity at risk... You must guard your integrity as if it's your most precious leadership possession, because that is what it is." Do what's right, make LIFER decisions!

I recall another time when I had to utilize the LIFER principle. I was faced with terminating a team member while working in retail cellular sales. Let me give you some background. It was the end of the 3rd Quarter and I had to make a decision that was sure to impact my organization one way or another— positively or negatively. Please believe me when I say that you do not want to make a decision that is going to have a negative impact on your team going into the 4th quarter of any retail establishment as this is the busiest time of the year. I had an employee that was up to be terminated however, he had a loyal customer base at my location. In addition, he was a Spanish speaker in a highly populated Hispanic area. He had good sales performance and was on track for the regionally recognized Sales Award. The 4th quarter was starting in another week, and the next generation of the Iphone was going to launch. There is no doubt that the store was about to get real busy. When I say real busy, I mean really busy. What should I do? If I terminate him I will definitely be impacted because firstly, he's a Spanish speaker, and secondly, I doubt I will be able to backfill his position because it is the 4th Quarter. If Human Resources does approve it, then it will probably take at least a month to effectively go through the hiring process. There is no doubt by terminating this employee, an important player on my team, it would jeopardize sales. Furthermore, I myself was up for the Regional Sales Recognition Award this year as well. I could easily sweep this under the rug, turn my cheek, act as if his poor time management behaviors (absenteeism & lateness) and poor attitude did not exist. Surely, it would be more probable that I would get the Sales Recognition Award if I keep him on my staff. Or would I? What would you do? I terminated him going into the 4th quarter and performance by my other representatives actually increased because they saw that I was one who lived by accountability. Sure, I lost the opportunity to get the personal recognition that I definitely wanted and deserved, but the long-term success of the team was and will always be more important to a true leader. Catapult leaders do not trade short-term convenience for long-term inconvenience; they do just the opposite. The LIFER principle led me to sacrifice.

GO GET YOUR CROSS!

Leaders have to sacrifice. I made the decision to sacrifice being down headcount, getting the sales recognition, and being understaffed for the good of the team. I knew deep down in my heart that, although other team members did not bring it to my attention, they saw the behaviors and they were counting on me to address them. The consequence of not sacrificing would have been far greater than keeping that employee on my team because I would have lost respect and the ability to hold my team accountable. In the end, everything turned out all right. I received not one but two additional employees two weeks later and to my astonishment, both were bilingual. Now, I have the respect of my team, I have additional staff members, and sales did not suffer. Sounds like a Win-Win-Win, situation for me!

Sacrifice is synonymous with leadership. As a leader, one has to be willing to accept the fact that he will not be able to do some things that he used to do, say things that he used to say, and socialize with some people that he used to socialize with. Accept it or not, being a leader obliges one to a higher standard not only in the work environment, but also in one's home community. A leader has to recognize this before he assumes the role of leader. If a leader is unwilling to sacrifice then I would highly recommend that he not take on a leadership role. During my many years in leadership, I have seen many talented, well capable leaders fall by the way side and sacrifice their careers instead of sacrificing their peers. I worked with a very good leader that was being groomed to be a more influential leader. In other words, upper management recognized his leadership aptitude and was willing to invest in him to eventually take on a position with greater responsibility. He was tasked with leading the #1 producing store in the South that consistently produced within the top 10 in our company of over 2,000 retail locations. What a great opportunity right? For sure, if he does well at this location, he will have the ability to write his own check. Well, while at this top notch location he decided to have a team builder where alcohol was ingested. After the team builder he gave a ride to one of his subordinates but both had been drinking. He was subsequently stopped by a law enforcement officer and received a DUI. Upper management found out and removed him from the top location and put him in one of the worst producing locations. Where did he go wrong? He sacrificed his career for a peer! You see, character is built through many acts but can be lost with just a single one!

Like it or not, as a leader you will be looked on as the first person to sacrifice. This is a good way to gain buy-in from your team because it shows that you are willing to do what is necessary to win. On the other end of the spectrum, if you, as the leader, are unwilling to sacrifice, then how can you ask others to sacrifice? Sure you can demand it, however, remember what John C. Maxwell told us about demanding. I can tell you from experience that you will have a very tough road ahead of you.

PROFESSIONAL DISTANCE

What is professional distance? One of my mentors introduced me to this concept. I would define this term as the distance where objectivity and dignity are preserved. One of the most important qualities of a great leader is his or her decision making ability. Two of the most important things that assist with the leader's ability to make sound decisions are his or her objectivity and dignity. If the leader is not seeing through a clear lens or an objective lens, and things are blurring his/her vision, then the best possible decisions will not be made. It is awfully hard to hold someone accountable at work if you socialize every weekend with him. Also, if your dignity is compromised because this distance is taken lightly, productivity at the job suffers because you are not taken seriously. This is why it is critical that a leader maintain his or her professional distance. Leaders must say what they mean and mean what they say. Not only this; their actions must support this. It is vital to preserve and maintain this professional distance.

While, in no way am I sexist, I must admit that males need to pay special attention to this. Not to say that it does not apply to the ladies, however, it has been my experience that males need to take heed. Do not mix business with pleasure. There is never a good time for business to mingle with pleasure. The outcome is always bad. I have seen some very good and tenured leaders lose their jobs because they wanted to flirt with the fire. We are all human and will on occasion be tempted. Just don't fall into the temptation. As I stated previously, all it takes is one act to jeopardize one's character. Think with the right head!

LEADERS DEVELOP OTHER LEADERS

Peyton Manning is arguably the most prolific Quarterback in NFL history. It seems that no matter what players you put around him, he made them better and found a way to win. There have been numerous times when "no name" players have gained tremendous recognition because of the leadership of this one leader. Leadership is about making others around you better. Furthermore, by making others around you better, you, the leader, will be rewarded with the deserved recognition. It doesn't work the other way around. Wanting to be the star and only wanting to see your name in lights is not a recipe for success. Remember, recognized leaders know that the reason they are recognized is because they have a good following of reliable people. They are nothing without their people. Period.

Invest time and energy in your people. Leaders recognize that everyone has leadership ability. Perhaps you say to yourself, "I once knew this problematic, negative, and always pessimistic person. There is no way that he/she could lead other people." I beg to differ. That problematic, negative, and always pessimistic person can lead others to take on the same qualities. Hence, their leadership ability. I call these individuals leaders because they have the ability to influence the behavior of others. The challenge is to develop these leaders to lead in a way that is encouraging, positive, and optimistic. The way you do this is by investing time in them, showing their value to the team, and developing them. I once had an employee that every time my assistant made a decision that he did not like, he would go and rally the rest of the team to build energy around something that was important to him. This caused division amongst my team because some let his negative attitude and views infect them and others did not. One day, I pulled him into my office and I asked him a few important questions, "Why? Why do you feel the need to spread your personal feelings with the team? Is this in the best interest of what our goals are and accomplishing them?" By asking him these provocative questions, he was able reflect and see the impact that he was having on the team. I went on to say, "You have great leadership ability", he looked at me like, yeah right! I replied, "look at who you are influencing. I bet you if you change it up, show buy-in, and be more positive, so will they. Can we try it?" He replied, "yes." Ever since that day, he was a positive influence on my team and the team as a whole improved. When there is a cancer, you must eliminate it immediately. This does not always mean that you have to terminate someone, but terminate the behavior that is not compliant with productivity and positivity.

Developing leaders also means that you have to develop your management team. I personally learned the importance of developing the leadership team. Every time I would go on vacation, my location's productivity would suffer drastically—to the point of night and day! This situation can be analyzed in two ways. Could it be possible that I was the one driving the productivity and that I was the most influential, tooting my own horn? Or did I not spend enough time developing my leadership team so that my location would run without skipping a beat in my absence? I choose to side with the latter and think that I did not pay enough attention to ensuring that my leadership team had an influence that would sustain them in my absence. It is for this reason that I created the leadership DEED of Trust.

DEED OF TRUST

The Deed of Trust is a tool widely used in the real estate profession that ensures that the property is "real" when purchasing land or a home. It essentially empowers the lender to make the decision to give the borrower a loan by verifying that the property is "real". It is a method of security. Sorry to deviate, but my use of the Deed of Trust has absolutely nothing to do with real estate. The Deed of Trust is an acronym that I developed which empowers leaders to lead and assists leaders in developing their people.

Nowadays in business, the word empowerment is thrown around like a hot potato. What does empower really mean? Is it just some word that we throw out there to make people feel good and to promote the concept of being a "business owner" to increase ownership of customers' issues? So, you ask the question, what is this DEED acronym that I speak of? Well the first D is for...

Develop

A leader must be committed to developing people all around him/her. This includes those that report directly to him, those that they report to, and their peers. A great sense of camaraderie emanates when people know that you want to develop them into something more than what they are or that you have a vision for them that they did not see for themselves. Furthermore, a sense of pride comes from knowing you have someone in your corner who wants the best for you. A leader must show that he/she has a vested interest in the development of others no matter what their title and that he genuinely cares about their growth.

The E is for....

Empower

Empowerment is one of those words that has been thrown around in corporate America which I refer to as "sound good jargon." Let me give you an example. A manager may say, "Sheri, I empower you to make the decision or Sheri is empowered to make that decision". Managers believe and have been taught that empowering gives a true sense of ownership to the employee and automatically flips that employee into "business owner mode". "Business owner mode" is what all organizations want their employees to envision themselves as. It is the mode that employees get in when they feel like their decisions have an immediate and profound impact on the business unit as a whole. At the end of the day, businesses see breakthrough results when people at the frontlines have this sense of business ownership. In order to empower, you must take the necessary time to develop the employees to make sound business decisions. It has always been amusing to me that organizations throw around the word empowerment but when a decision is made by the one who is so called "empowered" he or she is questioned on why the decision was made. True empowerment comes with one being educated about the right decision, at the right time, under the right circumstances. If a leader and his subordinates are asked the same question or faced with the same problem and their solutions are not in alignment, then empowerment does not exist. It takes time and energy to empower. Empowerment cannot be just as simple as saying, "go, you're empowered!"

The other E is for....

Engage

All parties have to be present, participating, and have a purpose; I call it the 3 P's. Although engage is the third letter in DEED, it is the most important. There is no development, empowerment, and delegation if people are not engaged. How do people get engaged? When they know that they bring value to the team/organization. How do they know that they bring value? Their leader not only tells them, but shows them how they add value to the organization every day. I repeat every day! How do you show your employees that they add value?

And the last D is for....

Delegate

When I assumed my first corporate leadership role I was told that delegation was the key to succeeding. I firmly believe this is true. Delegation helps one prioritize his day and not get bombarded with the petty stuff that is inconsistent with growth and productivity. This is wrong! If you think this is what delegation is, you are wrong! If you think delegation is receiving a request from another department and pushing it on a direct report to take care of it for you because you don't have the time, you are wrong! Delegation is a form of development and that is how it needs to be viewed. As a leader, identifying someone with talent and delegating more responsibilities to them as a developmental tool, will bring greater success. Delegating, warrants a greater standard of responsibility and accountability from the leader who is delegating the work because, in essence, if they are delegating correctly, they are giving themselves more work. Now, do not spend time focusing on "more work". It does not mean that you will have to spend an additional ten hours at work a week, but what it does mean is that you will be doing more fertilizing. You see, I think of delegating as walking around the office and identifying areas that need growth. In one hand there is a pitcher of water and in the other hand the seeds. Yes, as the leader, you will have to follow-up, coach, direct, provide constructive feedback, and hold accountable those that you delegate work to. When it is all said and done, you will have a team that will be loyal to you because you were loyal to them.

YOU CANNOT FORCE PEOPLE TO LEAD!

Ladies and gentlemen, you cannot put someone in a leadership role or force someone to lead if they have no desire to lead and expect them to engage in a high-level of leadership. Time in position, individual achievements, or being a top individual contributor do not determine leadership ability. There are reasons why people spend years upon years in their positions; they're satisfied! There are reasons why people are great individual contributors; because they only care about their performance! Please note that this is not bad—similarly in sports there are different positions and each has a role to play. However, forcing or naturally progressing someone into a leadership role who is either satisfied or selfish is a recipe for disaster.

TRUE STORY: As a manager in a retail location I worked with a very good individual contributor that had been employed with the company for three years in the same title. A re-organization was about to happen and my District Manager at the time asked me about this individual and the possibility of promoting him to a leadership role in another location. For literary purposes let's call the representative "Mack" and the District Manager "Doc." Doc said, "Jason, what do you think about promoting Mack to a leadership position?" I said, "You know Doc, Mack is a great individual contributor, however, I do not see the leadership characteristics necessary to make others around him better. For one, he's lazy and two, he only cares about his performance." Doc replied, "You know what Jason, it's about time for Mack to step up and take on greater responsibility." Next thing I know Mack is promoted to a leadership role in another location and 4 years later he is still a good individual contributor, satisfied, has a lackadaisical attitude with no sense of urgency, and still doesn't make others around him better. In his own words, "taking on a management role will be more work and less money". For the past four years he has stifled the growth of other employees that want to get promoted to leadership roles because he occupies the position needed for them to progress with no desire to lead. Good Choice?

APTITUDE VS. POTENTIAL

Let us begin by defining aptitude to lead and the potential to lead. An individual's leadership aptitude is his or her innate ability to lead. If an individual has a high leadership aptitude it is more likely that he/she will succeed in a leadership role with a faster return on investment or faster timeline to impact.

An individual's leadership potential is just that; his or her potential qualities or abilities that may be developed and lead to future success or usefulness. The keyword here is may. Have you ever looked at an individual and said, "He or she has so much potential!" What is potential if it is never realized? I believe it is similar to having knowledge without applying it. Growing up in New York, I saw many good basketball players with the potential to be great and to make it to the NBA. What is the difference between those that make it and those that do not? It is aptitude, hard work, and persistence. Sure in some cases it may be luck or who you know, however, I am a firm believer that luck is where preparation and opportunity meet. That little thing sitting on one's neck (in some cases it is big) that controls attitude is where the rubber meets the road. At the end of the day, it is one's Aptitude for positive Attitude.

See Doc either hired Mack into leadership because he believed in natural progression or that Mack had potential. Is there such a thing as natural progression? Does one have to want to progress in order for natural progression to occur? Remember, individual contributors have their places.

Do not force them to take on responsibilities that they do not want to take on. Sure, as a leader, you want to challenge and help your followers realize a higher level or gear that they never envisioned for themselves, but be wise in your decision making.

TAKE A LOOK INTO THAT PUDDLE

As a leader, self reflection is very important. Being brutally honest with yourself and consistently challenging yourself to be a better leader is key. You

cannot lead others if you do not lead yourself. Would you follow someone who lacks discipline, direction, or someone who has no control over his emotions? As the lyrics of the late Michael Jackson's song state: "It starts with the man in the mirror." Often times, we can be so consumed as leaders and not see ourselves as others see us. Take this for example. One day I had the pleasure of doing a presentation before my peers, leadership team, and mentor. Historically, I have been a very confident individual and sometimes that confidence comes across as cockiness to those who do not know me. After I presented my material, I asked my mentor "So Diane can you see it? Can you see me doing what you do?" She replied, "Yes I see it and you did well but I'm going to ask you a question that doesn't need answering (Diane is big on provocative questions). She said, "Are you doing it for yourself or for the people that you're going to lead?" Wow, talk about a brain buster. What could she possibly mean? She went on to explain, "you already have a presence because of your stature where you don't have to over compensate." She went on to say that it is neither good nor bad but it is just a different road that I would have to travel. You see that overcompensation came across as me lecturing or giving the impression that I knew it all. My goal is to lead people and have an impact on their lives that is measurable through the experience and knowledge that I possess; not to simply lecture material and come across as tooting my own horn. Taking a look into the puddle is a continuous exercise that catapult leaders will always have in their repertoire and has become a staple in mine.

LSC

Bestselling author of *The Ultimate Question*, Fred Reichheld, said by asking one question, "How likely is it that you would recommend this company to a friend or colleague?" (Net Promoter Score), organizations can increase customer loyalty, profits, and realize true growth. I would like to take Fred Reichheld's NPS concept to the leadership arena. To be consistent, I will keep the theme and call it the Leadership Survey of Clarity or LSC. I use the word clarity because the survey is very implicit with the name of the surveyed leader being used and will give clarity to a leader on how he/she is viewed. For example, the LSC asks four questions. Would you recommend Jason Montanez as a leader? Would you go the extra yard for Jason? Would you go the extra mile for Jason? Why/Why not? As previously stated, a key ingredient of leadership is self reflection and a good leader must ask himself the question, "Would my subordinates, peers, or superiors recommend me to lead others on a consistent basis?"

LSC, unlike NPS where one can give a score of either Promoters, Passives, & Detractors, requires that participants choose either Yes or No as an answer. The LSC question is closed for a reason. Think about it. If you were going to recommend someone for a leadership position, would you promote someone you were "on the fence" about to a subordinate, peer, or superior? I hope not. I hope you are absolutely sure of who you would recommend because if he or she does not turn out to be what you recommended, your credibility will be on the line. For an example of the Leadership Survey of Clarity please visit **leadsellcare.com**.

ARE YOU A PLAYER OR A COMMENTATOR?

In business, there are two types of workers: Players & Commentators. Players are those that make things happen. These are people that "be about it" and don't talk about it. Furthermore, the actions do the talking with Players and all they have time for is getting in the trenches and playing the game; any unproductive activity that is not conducive to getting the job done is asinine to a player. Players lead organizations in the right direction because they have a high sense of urgency and pride themselves in executing flawlessly. Organizations need Players to Win!

Commentators are exactly what they are; talkers. All they do is talk about the game. Commentators play the sidelines and pride themselves in observing and dissecting what is going on. In some cases, the commentators are the self proclaimed experts that have all the right answers but never share. Commentators usually hold their positions for a long time and are comfortable where they are. Additionally, they seldom take on new challenges because this will take away from their commentating time. Ironically, commentators are leaders too; they influence others to join the unproductive commentating party. There are players and commentators at every level of the organization. Some people are just players and some are just commentators; that is just the way they are and you cannot change them. However, there are those that are on the fence. I call these people "on the bubble." That is because they are highly influenced and right on the threshold of going in either direction of being a player or a commentator. If we were talking Net Promoter Score (NPS) these workers are those that are passive or those that do not know in which direction to go. It is in an organization's best interest to cultivate a culture of players and not commentators. It is imperative that on decision day or "D Day" those "on the bubble" workers are influenced so strongly by the players that it is clearly a no-brainer to stray away from the commentators. They must be forced to recognize that commentating will put them in one place and one place only; on the sidelines.

POSITION MEANS DIDDLY!

In John C. Maxwell's 360 Degree Leadership, He says, "Leadership is about disposition not position." You see my father holds a very high position in the family tree and my 3 year old son holds a very low position, however, I contend that recognition of leadership starts at a very young age. Take this for example: My dad has always been a disciplinarian. As a matter of fact, being a disciplinarian and a figure of authority was what he was to me growing up. There was really no emotion or cuddly-feely type of relationship between

us. My dad demanded respect but did not command respect. There is a difference. You see, Rapper/Entrepreneur 50 Cent said in one of his raps, "Respect comes from either admiration or fear." My dad demanded respect from me by trying to instill fear. That did not work. As I am a father now and my children are around my father, I see the same cycle occurring. He wants to be a leader and wants my children to follow his lead, but instilling fear and demanding respect because he is at the top of the family tree is just not working.

In my culture (Dad Puerto Rican and Mom Haitian), it is a sign of respect to say Good Morning and greet an elder with a kiss on the cheek. One morning, my youngest son JonJon (3yrs old) came into the kitchen and said good morning to everyone except my father. My dad said to JonJon in a forceful tone, "Say good morning to me, I'm Grandpa!" JonJon proceeded to walk away without saying a word. When I asked my son why he had not said good morning to Grandpa he replied, "Grandpa is mean!" You see, my dad was attempting to lead by position and was failing to get the desired result. There are no long-term positive outcomes when one leads by position. Sure, respect may be shown in your presence in the form of a handshake or another act of acknowledgement, but then behind your back your name gets thrown in the dirt. Think this does not happen? Is that true respect? Does one talk behind another's back if true respect exists? True respect is synonymous with discipleship in the sense that respect is given in and out of the presence of the leader.

YOU'RE AS STRONG AS YOUR STRONGEST LINK

It has been proven that if organizations want to realize breakthrough results in a time sensitive manner then it is in their best interest to leverage the strengths of their human capital. Early in my career, I used to look for the bottom 20% of my staff in any metric and instruct them to focus on their weaknesses to get better. Furthermore, I even made those that were weak subject matter experts in the metric where they were losing with hopes that they would improve. It was my hope, that by giving them added exposure to a metric that they were struggling in and creating a sense of ownership over this metric, success would result. In other words, it was my strategy to focus on the bottom performer because my thought process was that by focusing on him/her it would boost my results. The team is as strong as the weakest link right? To give you an example, I had an employee that struggled with his small business penetration. He was very strong in all other metrics but he just did not excel selling in the small business arena. So, what I did was make him the subject matter expert for small business. The subject matter expert would be the specialist for the team and be the "go to guy" when the team needed assistance with small businesses. I thought this would give him a sense of pride and provide a significant challenge for him since he excelled in all other key performance indicators. Naturally, with more emphasis and attention to a specific metric came better results for him, but it was not the results that I was looking for from the team; they were mediocre at best. Holistically, I found that this strategy was not a poor choice when time was not of the essence, however, when you want results yesterday, you must leverage the strengths of your people.

During my childhood we had an event called field day which was a competitive event amongst the schools' 3 grades (4th, 5th, 6th). I remember this day being the most exciting day of my elementary years. As a matter of fact, I couldn't wait to compete against my classmates. Did I mention I was very competitive? Field day was the Super Bowl of elementary. There were events like the cross country run, the fifty yard dash, and my favorite; the tug of war. The tug of war was my event because we were the undefeated champs and in 6th grade we were going for the 3rd consecutive year. I was pumped. It was my time to shine. As an overweight, somewhat athletic elementary student, I was dubbed as the anchor (the one who is always in the back). It had been our strategy in past years that the heaviest, strongest person (me) would be anchor. It had worked in the past, why change it now? The tug of war was always the last event because it was the most team oriented event and all grades could watch and cheer on their respective grade teams. This was without a doubt the pinnacle of field day. So, here we are, time to defend our title and ride off into the sunset as the undefeated tug of war champs. My grade team, now in 6th grade, lined up the same way we had for the previous two years. We had the strength in the back and the less strong at the front, after all, we had won this way the previous two years and this is the way we were taught; put your strength in the back. To our astonishment, the 5th graders lined up in the exact opposite position than we did; their biggest and strongest students were towards the front. I thought to myself, we're going to beat them easily. This victory was surely in the bag. I was wrong, the whistle blew and their big strong people (their strength) pulled with all their might and got my weaker frontline peers off balance; they now had the leverage. As my peers on the frontline tried to regain their footing I hunkered down and pulled with all my might, but it was not enough to overcome the concentrated effort of the 5th graders with their strength being in the front. After about 30 seconds of pulling with all our might, it was over. The 5th graders won by leveraging their strength and putting their strongest links in the front. Get your strong links and put them in the front. They will help your other links become stronger and breakthrough results will occur much faster.

WHAT ARE THE THREATS TO LEADERSHIP?

One of my group projects in undergrad at the University at Buffalo was based on the concept of employee sabotage. Why would someone engage in adverse behavior against their leadership, colleagues, or direct reports? We found that there is a greater probability of employee sabotage if the employee has been previously treated unfairly, they do not feel like their ideas are valued, or simply the law of reciprocity; if you don't do for me, I won't do for you.

Early on in my career I was gun ho about moving up the corporate ladder because I was under the impression that as I moved up, the complaining, the sabotaging, the backstabbing, the envy, and the jealousy would cease. After all, those that are promoted have the ability to only focus on the important things like teamwork, have the ability to separate emotion, and always have the best interest of the company in mind. I mean everybody that got promoted into leadership positions were professional, right? Man did I get a rude awakening! I remember sitting in a meeting and listening to what sounded like Kindergarten bickering and coming to the realization that being professional meant much more than the way one dressed. I mean, everyone looked really good in their business suits, but that was the extent of the professionalism on display at that particular meeting.

It is difficult to define the level of sabotage that I have witnessed in my corporate life. Fortunately, I have personally experienced very few instances. Sure, there was my boss who felt intimidated by me because of my education, and there was a time that a co-worker made it difficult for me to get something approved because I was selected for a position over him. As a wise man once told me, "You will always have haters as long as you are doing things right."

So, please take it from me:

- Don't hate, congratulate!

- Look & Act like a professional.

- Do what is best for the organization, not for yourself.

- Treat others with respect.

- When people need you, act with the same sense of urgency that would be expected if you were to ask something of them.

- Stay away from gossip and petty talk.

- Channel your energy to construct not destruct.

- You are not in High School anymore. It is time to bid farewell to childish ways.

- Do not get super emotional to the point where it affects your decision making process.

No one is perfect. Organizations face the same issues when dealing with people because people will be people. It is for this reason that leadership is so very important. The main point is that organizations do not succeed without effective collaboration between people. When sabotage occurs, leadership, and image suffer. The end result is a poor customer experience. And what usually happens as a result of bad customer experiences? I am sure all of you can do the math. Speaking about image...

HIT THE GYM

Charisma is a very important part of leadership. As a matter of fact, often times, people will follow a charismatic leader with little or no substance rather than following a non-charismatic leader with substance. Furthermore, a great part of charisma is physical appearance. Being physically fit is of the utmost importance not only for being healthy, but for gaining an advantage when leading and inspiring people. I ask the question, "How can you expect to lead, inspire, preach focus, discipline, and self-control if your appearance depicts a lifestyle that is contrary to your message? Where does your credibility go? How does this impact your ability to lead?" Now, I do not believe that if a person is overweight he/she cannot be a solid leader. What I do believe, is that if you show the same discipline, focus, sharpness in your appearance, it will be a whole lot easier to lead or be chosen to lead. I am pretty sure that there have been times when a hiring process came down to two highly qualified candidates and the determining factor was the ability for this person to be the "face" of the company or if they had the "look" or not. People buy from, listen to, and follow people they like; more often than not, who are physically appealing. Do yourself a favor and give yourself a competitive advantage, get active and look good! Invest in your appearance.

When I say invest in your appearance, I'm referring to caring about the way you present yourself to others, not necessarily spending hard earned cash. Nothing tells more than the care and preparation that one takes in his appearance. You want people to take you seriously, correct? I've heard of figures that 80%-90% of communication is nonverbal. What this basically means is that people will formulate an opinion based on one's overall appearance. One does not have to shop at Gucci, Prada, Louis Vuitton, or Chanel to be presentable so, do not go and break the bank, but do (I know some may think this is elementary, but believe me it's worth reiterating):

1. Make sure your clothes are ironed.

2. Make sure you are well groomed.

3. Make sure your clothes fit.

4. Exercise proper hygiene.

Another component to enhancing one's appearance is getting plenty of rest. It's amazing that when we incorporate exercise into our daily lives, we sleep better, have more energy, and just feel better. A huge part of leadership is having the self confidence to lead. People want to follow a leader that feels good, looks good, and has energy. Think about it. Would you rather follow someone who is bawling in his sorrow or someone who is confident because he feels and looks great? Get some sleep.

In no way will appearance supplement performance. To be a successful leader, a Catapult Leader, it is critical to have both. Looking good and performing well is a powerful combination. You can write your own ticket so to speak. I will never forget my first couple of days in corporate America during orientation, the human resources manager gave the new-hire training class the advice that, "You should dress for the job that you want, not the job that you have." While, I personally did not follow this to a tee, I do know that, like auditioning actors, playing the part does help in getting the part.

FORGET ABOUT TIME MANAGEMENT

Time is the greatest equalizer because no matter what, everybody is working with the same time. There may be different time zones but the fact still remains that there are 60 seconds in a minute, 60 minutes in an hour, and 24 hours in a day. It's easy and factual mathematics like the book cover. It should be easy if everybody is working with the same numbers right? Oh no my friends it's not easy because everyone has different situations and responsibilities. For example, the single mom that has to leave work no later than 5pm to then be a full-time mom after work really does have less time or should I say downtime than the recent college grad that can go to happy hour and various social events five times a week. That being said, this is why it is so important to forget about time management. Answer these questions: Do you have the ability to start and stop time? Does everyone have the same 24 hours in a day? Do you have timeouts that you can call throughout the day? The reality is that if you are not a coach, a referee, or you are not clocking someone's 40 yard dash, then you probably cannot manage time. It is not about attempting to manage something that you have absolutely no control over, but managing what you do have control over; yourself. Moreover, it is about leading and influencing your behavior throughout the day. Have a plan for yourself. And stick to it. Again, if you cannot lead yourself, how can you expect to lead others? Stop talking about time management and start focusing on self-management. This is a huge differentiator as successful leaders have the same time in a day as those that are unsuccessful.

Previously the importance of appearance was discussed. Let me make it perfectly clear that it does not matter how confident you are or how well dressed you are if you show up late. I'm talking about showing up late for peers, subordinates, and superiors. Your peers will talk about you as the person who is always late, your subordinates won't care if they're late because you are always late, and to your superiors you will be regarded as someone who cannot take on any added responsibilities because no matter how well you perfom, the little things like coming to a meeting on time are not adhered to. Later on I refer to tardiness as one of my all-time pet peeves. So:

1. Always plan for traffic.

2. The meeting always starts 10 minutes before the actual start time.

3. Always leave a half hour to an hour between commitments.

4. Be on time and ready.

The DEED of Trust, which we previously spoke about, is vital to forgetting about time management and improving self-management. You will have to put the work in initially to develop, empower, engage, and delegate, however, this will eventually free up time for yourself. Prioritizing in conjunction with the DEED of Trust is essential. Ask yourselves these questions to help in self-management.

1. What are the mission's critical points that need to get done?

2. When do they need to be done?

3. Why do these items need to be done?

4. Who has strengths that can help in getting things done?

5. How will I get this done?

Later in the Sell section, you will see how this resembles my current events assignment. It will all come together. It's all about bringing it back to basics. It's not complicated, we as humans make things complicated. Furthermore, the end result will be self-reliance by all, less stress, less long days at work, more time with the family, and better self-management.

THE ?

Are leaders born or made? The answer to this question is YES! Everyone is a leader in some capacity of his/her life. There are instances in their lives where they are leaders and where they are followers. As stated previously, leaders must have the ability to know when to lead and when to follow; this is a part of A&A that we discussed earlier. Let me give you an example. At work Johnny is a frontline employee and is not really regarded as a leader. He usually stays to himself and does a good job, but he is not a stellar performer. As a matter of fact, his managers do not consider him to be a leader because he is just not outspoken enough and just follows instructions like a good soldier. However, when Johnny is out of work, he is a totally different person. Johnny is a father of four, is the lead singer of a band that he put together, and on the weekends he takes his children to a local homeless shelter where they help prepare meals. Hmmm..., it seems as if Johnny does have some leadership qualities after all. Incidentally, if you ask anyone outside of work about Johnny he/she would say he is a natural born leader.

How possibly then could the people at work, specifically his superiors, not see the leadership qualities that Johnny displays outside of work? Well, no one ever asked or ever really got to know Johnny. Johnny has been a leader all this time and no one ever knew it. So, why does Johnny not take the same initiative at work that he does outside of work? There can be various reasons. Maybe Johnny does not feel valued at work. Perhaps Johnny does not believe in the current culture and direction of the organization. Maybe Johnny has had a poor experience with his boss which resulted in a lack of loyalty. Or Johnny does not see his employment as a career and he just looks at it as a job or a paycheck. Could it be that Johnny just doesn't care? We cannot disregard that possibility. Remember, you cannot force people to lead!

Then, there is Jessica. Growing up, Jessica's parents wanted her to play sports because they believed sports would teach her how to lead, work well with others, develop discipline, build up camaraderie, set goals, and hopefully inspire her to do more; but that was not her desire. You see Jessica was very shy as a young girl and always wanted to stay inside and not play with the other children her age until one day the unthinkable happened. Jessica's father signed her up for soccer. Scared as all hell, Jessica went to her first soccer practice and did not have a hunch what to do with the ball let alone where to actually kick it. All the other kids chuckled in disbelief. There was hope though. Standing at five feet tall was Coach Tiny. Coach Tiny got her nickname because most of the kids were taller than her yet she was a grown woman. Being a witness to the madness that Jessica was showcasing, Coach Tiny took the time to sit down with Jessica to breathe life back into a deflated body that felt defeated. Coach Tiny spoke words of encouragement like, "I believe in you", "I know you can do it", "I will help you", "We will do it together", and "You are not alone." Renewed by her words, Jessica found new life and together she and Coach Tiny practiced and practiced forming a solid relationship for years to come. Fast forward a couple of years. Jessica has now decided to be a coach because of the impact that Coach Tiny had on her. A once shy girl that never wanted to come out of the house, Jessica has now taken a leadership position giving guidance to others just as Coach Tiny gave her. When asked where her inspiration to coach came from Jessica answered, "I was not born a leader but because I had a great leader that believed in me, spoke words of encouragement, gave me a sense of direction, never left me to fend for myself, and was able to anticipate my needs, I choose to give back in the same capacity to lead and develop others." Jessica is an example of a leader that was made.

Often times, it takes a good leader to really look deep into another's soul and pull out the leader within him. It is sort of like the mantra of The Catapult Leadership Group "launching the leader within you." I am a firm believer that everyone has a leadership trait within him and with the proper skill, will, and understanding, one can be catapulted on a path to positively influencing others.

I'M NOT A SALESPERSON!

One of my sales leaders always used to say, "No one says that they want to be a salesperson when they group up!" He's right. When you are younger the top responses are Doctor, Lawyer, Policeman, an athlete, the president of the United States, or a superhero! It always baffles me when people do not consider themselves to be salespeople because of the negative-connotation that being a salesperson sometimes generates. But guess what? Every single person on God's green earth is a salesperson to some degree. You may not get paid like a salesperson, it may not be your title, and you may not have a quota; but, at some point in time, you will have to sell an ideology, a product, a service, and most importantly YOU! One of the constants in life is that if you're not selling, you won't be receiving. If you're not selling a vision then people will not follow, if you're not selling your product then people will not buy, and if you're not selling yourself then you won't get hired by an employer or an intimate partner. The great thing about being a great salesperson is that you don't have to sell.

TO SELL YOU DON'T HAVE TO SELL

Have you ever been at home after a long day of work and the phone rings but to your displeasure it is a telemarketer trying to sell you something? How did this make you feel? One of the most annoying things in the world is to be subjected to someone trying to sell you something just to sell it to you when you do not want to be sold anything. In order to sell, a conversation has to take place. The best sales people listen more than they speak and sell products and services they provide by catering it to the needs of the individual customer. People are different. If you give the same sales pitch to everyone then you will fail. The best sales people do not sell—they consult! This may be surprising to some but people actually know what they want. It is the job of the sales person to make the shoe fit.

I am a proponent of simplicity and not over thinking a process. Have you ever had a meeting about the meeting and then had another meeting to talk about that meeting? Often times, we think that solutions have to be in these profound acts when most often the answers are sitting right under our noses. All we have to do is ask the right questions. In middle school I remember we had a weekly assignment called "Current Events" to which many of you can relate. There were five questions that we had to answer for the assignment to be deemed complete. They were; Who? What? Why? When? & How? At that time, I did not think these five questions had much application to much more than my current events assignment, but in retrospect, they did. In my opinion, Current Events was a fairly simple assignment that allowed me to give a succinct analysis of an article by answering five questions. I believe that by asking these five questions in a sales environment, breakthrough performance will be the result. There's one kicker though. The positioning of these questions must be from a provocative stance. In other words, the questions must be used to bring about greater thinking; critical thinking. Furthermore, none of these questions can be closed. The reason for asking these types of questions is to get the prospective client to speak. Your job is to listen. Let's look at a few provocative questions using our "current events" model:

- Who in the organization would benefit from such a solution?

- What are you hoping to get out of this?

- Why am I here?

- When are you planning for this to happen?

- How is this impacting your business?

What other questions can you come up with? The main objective is to ask questions that evoke more than one or two word responses and involves thinking on behalf of your prospective client. Furthermore, this will lead you to their way of thinking, which in turn will allow you to play on the same level, and tailor your value based solution to their specific need.

BASS PRO SHOPS VS. JOHN DEERE

No, I'm not going to differentiate the product lineup of each company, however, I am going to illustrate that when shopping for tools dependent on the job and its specifications, one will choose to patronize either company based on being a Hunter or a Farmer. If you are a Hunter, there will be a greater likelihood that you will shop at Bass Pro Shops for equipment and if you are a farmer, then you will probably go to John Deere for equipment. Furthermore, at each respective location you will find different tools to get the job done whether you're a hunter or a farmer. In sales, there are two mindsets; Hunters and Farmers. Let me disclose that neither is the right way to sell. Whether one decides to be a Hunter or a Farmer, is dependent on a host of factors, the industry in which they serve, the time of the month, the clientele etc...Can one be a Hunter and a Farmer? Of course! It is best that one diversifies his portfolio and distinguishes when it is the best time to utilize each skill set. Let's first delve into Hunters.

HUNTERS: Seek sales. These are the sales professionals that have to cold call and seek; because if they do not seek, they will not find. Hunters are predominantly those that are purely commission based or that have a heavy commission component to their compensation structure. Specifically, they are those that have to go door to door, cold call, and will not eat if they do not get out and initiate things themselves. Furthermore, hunters have a very intense sense of urgency. Hunters are fueled by instant gratification and do not have the patience to wait; because waiting equates to starving. They are typically the best sales people and work very well under very demanding sales conditions. Relationships are not of the utmost importance to Hunters. They are more concerned with closing the sale. When you think of a hunter, what comes to mind?

FARMERS: The farmer is more focused on building relationships when selling. He/she who takes on this role does not put a major emphasis on closing the sale yesterday, rather giving the prospect the time to think it through and not be overbearing. The farmer is willing to sow now and wait for the harvest. In any case, the farmer is not overly concerned with making a quota or maximizing on monetary pay out. Farmers have faith and trust that the work they put in today will result in a reward for tomorrow. Furthermore, the farmer's sense of urgency is lower than that of hunters and is comfortable with allowing sales to come to them. Consumers feel more comfortable with farmers because they do not feel forced to make a decision immediately. In other words, they are given more breathing room. This is probably the more customer-focused approach or avenue one would take if the deal he/she is pursuing has a substantial impact on his bottom-line. A farmer must understand that he will have to have two to three more times the prospect list or funnel of the hunter to compensate for the lack of tenacity and the longer sales cycle. Nowadays, having solely the farmer mentality is not very prominent because of how competitive the landscape is. You literally will not eat if you are too late; there are too many options for consumers.

The best sales people know how to find the median and maximize on opportunities that warrant both hunter and farmer mentalities. It's not which one is better, rather which one do I have to use with this individual customer. Which will the customer be more receptive to? The only way to know this is through experience and leadership that can coach to it. So, which is the best ideology to undertake, the hunter or the farmer? It's both! I recommend that you shop at both to ensure that you have the proper tools for any situation; whether it be hunting or farming. The tools or equipment that you need to get the job done will determine whether you shop at Bass Pro Shops or John Deere.

MAX OUT ON OPPORTUNITIES

One of my bosses used to always call himself an Opportunist: He said that's what he was good at. When an opportunity presented itself he would always seize that opportunity. One day I went to a nationally recognized bank in America and wanted to get something notarized because this was a free service to account holders. The document that I needed notarized had my wife's name on it. The manager of the branch (the notary public) came and said, "who has the account with our bank? Is it you or your wife?" I replied, "I have the account with you all." She continued, "Well we can only notarize documents for the person that holds an account with us." I replied, "Ok thank you" and walked out. I'm sorry, I really don't have the time to argue back and forth with businesses on what's right or wrong; I just take my business elsewhere! What was this manager's missed opportunity? Yup you guessed it. The proper response would have been, "Customarily, we only notarize documents for account holders, however, we have a really great Checking/ Savings offering here that is very easy to set up and I can get that document notarized in no time." Or how about, "Well, why doesn't your wife have an account with us?" This may have uncovered an additional need to open an account. Or, seize the opportunity to plant a seed! "Customarily, we do not do this, however, I'm going to go ahead and take care of you just as if you were a customer because we would love to earn your business in the near future." It takes less than a minute to notarize a document with no cost associated! Would this have been worth the investment?

YOU'RE NOT A PSYCHIC, DON'T TRY TO BE ONE

In order to be successful in sales you cannot be afraid to spend other peoples' money. I have seen people psyche themselves out of sales because they "had a feeling the customer would say no" or "the customer looked like they didn't have money." Stop trying to be a psychic! What happened to Miss Cleo? You know the lady back in the day that would pop up on your television and utter the words "Call me now" in her made up Caribbean accent. Exactly my point! She was a fraud. Stop trying to be a mind reader. It's a lot easier and more lucrative to just simply engage in conversation. Have you ever heard of the saying "Go Hard or Go Home?" That's what you have to do in order to be a top salesperson.

I once had an employee named Dre. Dre did not have a commissioned sales history by any means and was really caught up in a transition where the organization was making a change to a universal strategy. This meant that all representatives would be commissioned and tasked with selling and not solely providing customer care as they had been accustomed to doing. When this change happened, Dre expressed his dissatisfaction with selling and lack of passion in influencing others to purchase a product or service. So what was Dre's issue? To put it short, Dre had a problem spending other people's money. Why did he have a problem spending other people's money? It was directly related to the value that he placed on the products or services that he was tasked to sell. You see, it is very hard to sell a product or service that you yourself would not buy because you do not see the value of it. It is similar to a Toyota salesperson driving a Cadillac. If you yourself do not believe in the product that you are selling and do not see the value, you will not be able to sell to your max. Dre also listened to others who talked about their struggles through the difficult economy and listened to news reports on how spending was down amongst consumers. While spending was down, the wireless industry, specifically Verizon Wireless, did not see the impact of the recession to the level that others did. When I would ask Dre why he didn't like selling he simply said, "We're in a recession and people do not have the money to buy. Plus, I just don't like selling to people." While we were in a recession, people did have money to spend because his peers were selling at a very high level and the store location showed positive year over year growth.

Dre was a very good salesman but he just didn't know it. He did such a great job selling himself on the idea that people did not have money that he could not overcome his own way of thinking. Additionally, Dre spent most of his time worrying about things that he could not control like the company moving to a "universal" model and trying to sell me on the idea that people are not spending money in the recession. If only Dre spent time thinking inside the box! While Dre was very passionate about the operational side of the business, I always told him that his way of thinking and his lack of adapting to the new business model would ultimately lead to his demise. Consequently, Dre was eventually promoted to a customer (fired).

TTS

Trash Those Stereotypes! Whatever stereotypes you may have need to be trashed. Whatever notion you may have about your customers prior to getting to know them, need to be thrown away. Whatever you were taught, experienced, or felt directly or indirectly needs to be placed in the garbage disposal. I cannot tell you how many times I have seen salespeople, including myself, miss out on sales and greater opportunities because they had some kind of preconceived notion about their customers before they even started getting to know them. Start on a clean slate with every new customer. When I say everyone I mean everyone. No Latino, White, Black, Indian, Asian, person is the same. No two are alike. Consider each person an individual. One has to have the courage and the ability to leave all prejudices at the door to truly uncover all opportunities that exist. Take this for example.

As a Leader, I pride myself as one that is very observant and hands on. In others words I look and touch a lot! LOL. Just joking. All kidding aside, I spent much of my time observing my direct reports and being in the trenches so to speak, with my people. Throughout this time I caught myself stereotyping and others doing the same. As a matter of fact, reminding people to TTS was one of the biggest challenges and opportunities to increase sales. No example resonates more than the case of the dumb, dirty, and dingy CEO. For story telling purposes, let's call him the ODB and no, it doesn't stand for the "Ole Dirty Bastard" one of the members of the 1990's Hip-Hop Super Group Wu Tang Clan. ODB stands for "Old Dirty Boss."

So, one day ODB came into our store location and as I often did, stood in the background to see how long it would take for a member of my team to welcome a customer with a smile. As a rule of thumb, I taught my representatives that all who entered the store needed to be acknowledged/welcomed within three seconds of entry. There is nothing worse than patronizing a location and your presence is not even acknowledged. Sorry, I digressed... back to the story. So, ODB with salt and pepper hair gets out of a Toyota Camry and enters the store. He is promptly greeted and I hear him asking to upgrade his basic phone. Without hesitation my representative says, "no problem" and proceeds to show ODB our selection of flip phones. As my salesman helped ODB, I'm thinking to myself, "Why isn't he showing ODB all of the smart phones, tablets, and other new technology we have to offer?" After all, I did give my team the directive to show the benefits of smart phones and tablets because this was the direction that the company was going. As my employee walked over to the inventory room to get a case for the basic phone that he just sold, I approached him for some OTSC (on the spot coaching). I asked, "So, what does ODB like about the smart phones?" My rep replied, "Who that old dirty guy? He doesn't even know how to use the basic flip phone that he has. Plus, all he asked to do was upgrade to a basic flip phone. Did you hear him speak? He sounds dumb!" (I actually did hear him speak and it sounded like he had a speech impediment). I replied "Ok, which tablet did he like most?" My rep replied, "Jay I know this guy won't buy a tablet, he won't even look at a smart phone." I said, "Ok, where does he work?" My rep replied laughing, "Are we looking at the same person? He probably doesn't even have a job. He's wearing sweat pants with holes in them, dirty sneakers, he's not shaven, and hopped out of a Toyota Camry." My rep had just bought a brand new Lexus so he thought he was hot stuff! So I said, "Interesting, I'm going to go introduce myself and get to know him." My rep replied, "Ok, but I bet you he won't buy a smart phone or a tablet!" Little did my rep know that I wasn't going to try to sell him anything. I simply wanted to have a casual conversation with hopes to uncover any additional opportunities.

As I approached ODB I extended my hand and said, "Good afternoon, sir my name is Jason Montanez, the store manager, and I wanted to ensure that you were getting great service today!" ODB replied in his very slow paced speech, "Everything is going well, thanks for asking." I replied, "Great! So you're not going to take the dive to a smart phone today, huh?" He replied with a smile, "I'm an old man that doesn't need to be smart. I just need my employees to be smart." Ding Ding Ding! Bells went off and I saw out of the corner of my eye my employee's eyes open wide like he just saw a ghost. I proceeded to say, "Nice, how many employees do you have?" ODB said, "About 750! I'm the owner and CEO of a software company. I also own two local banks". Whoa! With a grin on his face, ODB said, "You didn't think I was a CEO huh?" We went on to talk about how he easily moves millions in stocks, interest rates, and business in general. He went on to explain that he had a stroke some years back and that's why his speech was slow. Yeah ODB spoke slowly but he was very smart. He went on to give me the name of his COO and told us that their company was with a competitor of ours. He said, "give her a call and tell her that I told you to contact her. See what kind of deal you can give her." I looked at my employee and I had to snap my fingers to get him out of his trance. He was in total shock and disbelief.

So, what's the moral of this story? Yup, you've got it right! You have to TTS! You never know who you will be talking to. Why limit yourself and your opportunities by some predisposed stereotypes? I found it amazing that when someone came in dressed professionally in a shirt and a tie or a business suit, that there was a greater likelihood to have work conversations or ask the question, "What do you do for a living?" One thing is for sure, people enjoy talking about themselves and what they do. So why not ask? When I asked my employee why he didn't ask he said, "He didn't look like a CEO." How does a CEO look? How does one look like when he/she has money? If someone drives a BMW, Ranger Rover, Jaguar, Benz or any high end luxury vehicle does it mean that they have money? How do you know that they have a garage and driveway to park that vehicle? The answer is we do not have the answers to those questions. You are doing a disservice to yourself and your organization if you are blinded by stereotype shades. So, TTS!

RISE

As the sun rises every day, so will your sales when you incorporate the following into your day to day dealings. I have developed an acronym that will help anyone sell and close more business if they follow the RISE sales philosophy.

REVENUE: All businesses want to improve revenues. Center your probing questions on revenue for that top-line impact that all companies look for. This will help in developing a return on investment by giving a tangible number. A couple of questions to ask are, "What are your revenue goals?" or "How are you currently increasing revenues?" Then, tailor your solution to how you can help them make more money. You have to tell them how your solution will help them sell more!

IMAGE: How will your product or service increase your client's image? When people think of or experience your company, what picture does it paint? Nowadays, image is very important and those that are not seen in a positive light will surely fall behind. When I mention image, I am referring to how one is perceived in the industry by competitors, customers, and the whole supply chain. Something as insignificant as furniture makes a big difference. Visualize this: I am one who is always professionally dressed, likes the finest wines, and dines at the finest restaurants. I also am a decision maker at my company where we take the utmost pride in entertaining our guests when we invite clients to our office. I have two appointments in the coming weeks with competitors in their respective industries. The first company that I visit has a fold out table and folding chairs in the room where we are meeting (I'm talking about the ones like at Uncle Pookie's BBQ). The sales presentation was good but I was not overly impressed with their culture. A week later I went on an appointment with their competitor. I walked into the meeting room furnished with an oak wood table and ergonomic leather chairs similar to the type we have at our office. I was greeted with a glass of water and a coaster was strategically placed on the table where I sat. Both companies did an equal job in presenting their products/services, but only one will get my business. Which one do you suppose will get my business given that their sales presentations were equal? Image is important.

SERVICE: How will your product/service offer a solution to provide increased service to customers? Will your clients' customers be happier than before your product/service was used? It is important to find innovative ways to relate how your product/service is necessary to increase customer service! So, if I am selling copy machines, I am going to talk about the reliability and dependability of the product that I offer compared to the current product that they are using. Switching to my product, will result in less downtime, which will increase productivity, and product to the customer. In other words, customers will not have to wait resulting in an improved customer experience! We all know customers do not like to wait!

EFFICIENCY/EFFECTIVENESS: Business books talk about it, your boss talks about it, your customers holler it, and I'm still going to talk about it. Businesses are always looking for solutions that streamline their businesses and take any unnecessary costs/steps out of the equation. After all, this is the smart way to do business and one should tailor their sales strategy towards making their solution the most efficient and effective. This, in turn, will prove to be the most cost effective even if your solution has a higher price point. You, as the sales professional, need to relay this message and tailor it to your individual client.

Ideally, RISE should be used in its entirety to truly be impactful. However, you will notice that some people don't care about Image or Service and just care about Revenues. What you will notice is that every component of RISE relates to the other. If you increase your Efficiency/Effectiveness, it will have a natural impact on Service to the customer, which in turn will increase your Image, and will ultimately result in increased Revenues.

DON'T BE AN ASS!

I was once told that when you assume it can be construed that you make an ass–of–u–and–me. Assuming is the single worst thing that a sales person can do. Assuming does not allow you to uncover additional opportunities and can send you on a whirlwind in the wrong direction for even the initial opportunity. I learned a very valuable lesson when my sales leader Mike took our sales team through a sales exercise revolving around asking good uncovering questions. Mike said, "You all would say that you are top notch sales professionals right?" Our team answered with a resounding, "YES!" Mike went on to say, "And you would say that you're currently asking the right questions when you go on your appointments, correct?" The sales team answered once again with a resounding "YES." Mike said, "Ok, let's play a sales game. I'm going to give you a scenario and I want each of you to ask me a question to uncover who I am and what I'm doing... ready?" Sales team confidently said, "Let's go!" There were 10 people on our sales team. Here's how the conversation went:

Mike: I am at home wearing a mask. What am I doing?

Rep 1:   Are you on top of your roof?

Mike: No

Rep 2:   Do you have a ladder?

Mike: No

Rep 3:   Are you outside?

Mike: Yes

Rep 4:   Are you in the front or the backyard?

Mike: I'm not in my yard.

Rep 5:   Are you on the porch?

Mike: No

Rep 6: Are you in the Garage?

Mike: Nope

Rep 7: I got it! You're an exterminator?

Mike: LOL nope!

Rep 8: Is it a Halloween mask?

Mike: Nope. Two more reps left! Come on my professional sales team!

Rep 9: Does the mask cover your whole face?

Mike: Yes. It comes down to this last question!

Rep 10: What do you use the mask for?

Mike: I thought you would never ask! So the balls don't hit my face! I'm a baseball catcher. Get it? I'm at home as in home plate with a mask on!

The moral of the story is that we all thought we were excellent at what we did. We were well paid and recognized salespeople. However, we assumed. For the most part, we all assumed when he said he was at home that he meant he was literally at his house. Often times, we assume that what people are saying is what we interpret them to be meaning. Assuming can result in time wasted, looking like a fool, and ultimately affecting your bottom-line. All we had to do was ask, "What does home look like?" or "Why are you at home?" This would have saved us all from looking like asses!

4 "P's" AND A "C"

Now that we talked about RISE, I would like to give you a golden nugget to bring it all together. I call it 4 P's and a C. If this is followed, you will not only be successful in business, but in life as well.

PLAN:

We've all heard it before that, "If you don't have a plan, you're planning to fail" or some variation of this statement. Believe it or not, this statement is very true. If one does not have a plan how will he get to where he is going? This is why people create business plans when opening up a business, strategy sessions when one needs to tackle an obstacle, and project managers are in place to ensure project completion every step of the way. A plan is worthless without steadfast action. Once a plan is agreed upon, green means GO! Sure, there may be slight adjustments to the plan, but there should not be any major deviance. I have worked with many companies that had good plans in place to do something that would improve operational efficiency but a year later the plan did not come to fruition because of inaction. Sometimes, they had already invested in a software or equipment for this plan, but years later the plan had not been worked on. Work your plan! Former undisputed heavyweight boxing champion of the world Mike Tyson said it best, "Everyone has a plan until they get punched in the face!". Although you may get punched in the face along the way, do not let that stop you from working the plan. Bob and weave and make the adjustment; but, keep moving forward!

PROSPECT:

Always be prospecting (ABP). When I was a business account executive our leadership team wanted us to prospect from 9am–11am every day. While this is a good strategy, prospecting needs to be happening all day long even when you're "off." The reason behind this is that you never know who you will meet and where you will meet them. That guy at the end of the bar could be the decision maker that could potentially get you paid. That person in front of you at the checkout line could know the person who could help you start the business that you have been dreaming about opening. The Janitor that comes and picks up your trash everyday could have a brother who can introduce you to someone that could be your ideal partner in life. Just say hi and be friendly to everyone that you come in contact with. When doing this, you should not have an ulterior motive in mind but just do this to be nice. Make someone's day, show that you are open to conversation, and prospects will just magically begin to appear; Voilà!

Another part of prospecting is engagement. How engaged are you in the community in which you reside? What boards do you serve on? What organizations are you affiliated with? How often do you participate in professional networking events? This is just a list of questions one should ask to ensure that they ABP!

PROPOSE:

No, I'm not talking about getting down on one knee or giving any advice to whoever may think they are ready to tie the knot. What I'm referring to is to propose the value that you bring in building a relationship with the prospect. Why would they do business with you? What do you bring to the table? What differentiates you? What makes you unique? Is it good conversation? Do you have the same alma mater? Maybe you're originally from the same part of town and associating with you reminds them of some good memories. Find some form of commonality that allows you to connect on a personal level. People do business with people that they like. No matter what your product offering is, if they don't like you, then they will not do business with you. Be observant, listen attentively, and propose your value in building a relationship. Relationships get you to where you want to go. No one can do it all by himself. No one!

PROVIDE:

Now that you've shown your value it's time to show what's in it for them aka WIIFT. What problem are you solving by them doing business with you? What solution are you providing that will make them more efficient? How will you make their lives easier? How will you make them more money? Sounds a lot like RISE huh? Because it is! This is where RISE comes into play. This is where the marriage between 4P's and a C & RISE happens. Show the prospect that it is just common sense to do business with you and by not doing business with you is just incomprehensible.

CLOSE:

Early in my sales career I took pride in myself as being the closer. I felt there was not a person that I couldn't close. I mean, I felt that I could sell water to a whale and ice to an Eskimo. I often used to call myself Mariano Rivera (arguably the best closer in Major League baseball history and a New York Yankee) because that's just how confident I was and I am a New Yorker. I felt that you could put any one in front of me and I would be able to close the deal. To some extent I still feel this way. While I was a great closer, it didn't matter how good I was, if I didn't abide by the 4P's & a C; specifically the first two P's (Plan & Prospect). As one of my mentors once told me, "it doesn't matter how good of a closer you are if you don't have anything to close!" This is so very true!

Lastly, ask for the business! You won't be a good closer until you just ask for the business. Do not be afraid to ask for what you want. You want to date that beautiful woman, Ask! You want the business, ask for the business! Close the deal and ask! The end result will be a yes or a no! Do not be scared of rejection, it's part of life! Don't be scared of getting punched in the face, it is a part of life. Keep going, asking, and close!

IN ORDER TO CARE YOU ARE GOING TO <u>HAVE</u> TO <u>CARE</u>

Taking care of customers is nothing new to business. As a matter of fact, it is not ground breaking news that if you do not take care of your customers someone else will. So, if this is the case, why do companies still continue to struggle with customer care? We have heard the phrase stressed over and over again, "We would have no work, if it were not for our customers", or "The customer is always right" (I personally disagree with this). It baffles me that the mission and vision statements, the websites, the company t-shirts, and the marketing campaigns of so many organizations profess to provide dependable and reliable service to their customers yet, the actions of some of their employees are often times inconsistent with this stance. What is the issue?

Culture is the issue. Somewhere along the line the culture was not disseminated to everyone in the organization. The leadership did not do a good job of coaching to the message that care was the most important point. Please understand that caring is not giving customers everything they want. I agree that when in a for profit business, there must be a point where you cannot satisfy every single customer.

The hiring process must revolve around the care principle and somehow the interviewer will have to gauge if the person "cares." Does this person have pride about truly caring for the customer? Does he or she have a "can do" attitude? What do they personally care about? Leaders must tailor their interview questions around revealing what makes this person tick and his/her own personal care level.

A concept that I studied in grad school and which I've heard thrown around corporate America is EQ instead of IQ. EQ refers to the concept of Emotional

Intelligence and a person's ability to connect on a personal and emotional level to influence behaviors and drive results. I recommend that everyone Google "Emotional Intelligence" and spend time reading and applying the research that Daniel Goleman has done on this important concept. Emotional Intelligence is a key ingredient in Caring.

CUSTOMER SATISFACTION IS WORTHLESS!

The days of customer satisfaction are gone. If you're looking to satisfy your customers then you're losing. The current business climate calls for getting your customers to become loyal to you not just satisfied or happy. What this means is that no matter what a competitor does or says, even if the consumer will be saving money by switching to a competitor, they will not even consider it. This is what's called consumer loyalty. It is quite easy to create customer loyalty and it is a shame that more customer loyalty does not exist. Really, only four things are necessary:

1. Provide a reliable product/service (add value).

2. Do what you said you were going to do (Keep your Word).

3. Answer your phone when customers call. In other words, be there for them when they need you.

4. Resolve any issues/concerns with the same urgency as if it were your problem.

As stated earlier, simplification is key. We do not have to over think things. This is not rocket science but a concept thought of a long time before you and I existed. The difference is discipline and who Cares enough to follow the four step model. Do you want to retain your customers and realize true growth? If the answer is yes, do not try to satisfy your customers; care for them!

EMPATHY VS. SYMPATHY

The ability to empathize is probably the most important aspect of Caring. It is awfully difficult to truly care and be genuine about it when empathy calls in sick. That does not mean feeling sorry for anyone or being sympathetic, but truly feeling what others feel. Those that see the world in black and white with no gray area have difficulty empathizing. The ability to empathize sometimes means that one must compromise or negotiate. Moreover, people that feel very passionate about certain subject(s) have a harder time empathizing or negotiating.

I am a stickler about being on time. When I conducted my staff meetings I would tell my employees that the one thing you could control was being on time. It was and still is my thinking that nothing tells me more if you care or not than if you are on time and prepared. I guess I get this from my college football coach that used to lock the doors five minutes before the meetings started. So, if the meeting started at 2pm, you had better be in your seat and ready to go at 1:55pm or else some hardcore discipline would commence (i.e. running all the stadium stairs at 5am). At the time, I thought my coach was being a hard ass, but when I entered corporate America and I saw people being passed over for promotions for the "little things", I became a believer. That being said, I had a zero tolerance policy for being late to staff meetings and to work. In other words, I had to learn to empathize with employees and compromise/negotiate with something that I felt so passionate about which was being on time. Nothing illustrates this more than in the case of my former employee Kanani.

Kanani is a single mother that was taking care of her ailing mother who had been recently diagnosed with cancer. One day Kanani was late for our weekly meeting and everybody knew that was a no, no. So, I waited until the meeting was over to have a conversation with her (I always prided myself on praising in public and coaching in private). I asked Kanani if everything was alright (because she was always on time) and she explained to me that she was taking care of her mother last night and didn't get much sleep. She pressed snooze when her alarm went off and went back to sleep causing her to be late. I went on to tell her that this will still count as a lateness occurrence and asked her if there was anything that I could do to help. You may be asking yourself, "Jason couldn't you have let that lateness slide given the circumstance?" Yes, I could have, however, I believe that when you're leading a team you must hold everyone to the same standard and demand that everyone be accountable. If you don't, it may be a recipe for failure or mediocrity because the other employees will have a sentiment that you play favorites. Kanani vowed never to be late again and apologized profusely. She then went on to ask me if accommodations could be made with her schedule to avoid being late because of the extenuating circumstances of her mother's illness. Here's when I had to empathize. Yes, I had sympathy for Kanani's situation because I could only imagine having a parent fight cancer (thankfully, I have never experienced that). Kanani expressed that her mom was her best friend and she did not know her dad. Moreover, Kanani was a good performing employee with a great attitude. So, what I did was collaborate with the other employees to make them feel involved in the process (the schedule was already complete and changes needed to be made that would impact them). Once everyone complied, I made the accommodations that Kanani requested. Her mother would lose the battle with cancer two weeks later. Although, I was sad that

Kanani had lost her mom, I was happy that the accommodations could be made for her to spend more time with her mom in her final days.

It may seem as a no brainer to make the accommodations for Kanani for some, however, I can tell you that it is not a no brainer because I have experienced managers not having any empathy in situations like this because the business "comes first". The business does not come first! There is no business without the employees. Businesses find solutions for complex problems all the time. If you want to retain your employees, the leaders must care enough and have the empathy to find the solutions to their employees' complex problems. If you want your employees to care about their customers, show them how to care through your actions in caring for them.

OFFENSE VS. DEFENSE

In order to care you have to know when to play each role. In sports the offense's purpose is to score and the defense is to prevent the opponent from scoring. If played right and well, defense leads to offense. This is no different when caring for customers.

Offense is being proactive and anticipating customer needs. When playing offense, you have the ability to turn a non sales transaction into a sales transaction. So, you score. On the other hand, defense is not as combative an approach as it may seem or preventing the customer from winning or getting over, but a way of taking ownership of a problem regardless of its origin. It is the art of preventing market share from churning and preserving the name and brand. It is simply defending the brand by owning the issue and promoting a world class customer experience. Let me give you examples of both.

When I was a call center supervisor, I always taught my employees to analyze the customer's account against issues that they had experienced with other customers. What I was telling them to do was play offense by anticipating the customer's needs and if we had the opportunity to stop a poor experience before it happened, we needed to make that happen. Most of the time, this type of service leads to sales opportunities and the "whoa" factor (to be discussed later on). Very seldom do you find a unique issue in customer care. For the most part, it is something we have seen before and there are outlined processes and procedures to handle such a situation. Nothing illustrates this better than what Veronica did for a customer when I was a retail store manager. One day, Veronica had a customer who just wanted to make a payment on her bill. When Veronica pulled up her bill to process the payment, she noticed that something was wrong. Based on her experience, she noticed that the customer was being billed incorrectly and proactively made the adjustments to avoid this from happening in the future. You see, Veronica could have just processed the payment and let the customer walk out the door happy as it was unbeknownst to the customer that she had been overpaying and was being billed incorrectly. When the customer noticed that Veronica was going above and beyond to help her, she became more receptive to the sales pitch that Veronica gave to her. Veronica said, "Now that we've got that resolved and we're saving you x amount of money, I noticed that your son doesn't have a phone. What if I told you I can give you a phone for your son and you would still be saving x amount of money than what you are used to spending?" The customer said, "You know, his birthday is right around the corner, sign me up!" What opportunities do you have in your organization to play Offense?

Now, let's talk about Defense. As stated earlier, defense is about preserving the brand and doing whatever it takes to ensure that the customer has a world class customer experience. If an organization plays great offense and their policies/procedures are customer focused with the intent to be proactive rather than reactive, the opportunity to play defense will be minimized. Defense usually occurs when the customer interaction is escalated. Remember, playing defense is not preventing the customer from scoring or getting over on the company. To truly care, one cannot have the attitude that it is the company against the customer and that it is a sign of weakness if concessions are made. The emotions must be removed and a state of objectivity and empathy must be present to play great defense. This is probably my most memorable experience of a company playing defense.

When I bought my Toyota Tundra, it was the end of the month and they were having a great sale. I went to the dealer after work so it was already late in the evening. By the time I test drove, negotiated, and signed the paperwork it was dark, the dealership had already closed, and I was very tired. I must admit, I didn't check the vehicle as well as I should have because I just wanted to get out of there. The next morning, I noticed a deep gash in the wood grain of the steering wheel. It was obvious that buffering or sanding the steering wheel down would not be enough to resolve this cosmetic fault. I said to myself, "I can't believe I missed this detail. I'll get around to it early next month because it's the end of the month and I need to ensure that I personally close the month out strong with my sales commitments." Once the month ended, I went back to Toyota and explained the situation to a really nice gentleman in the service department. I said, "Sir I just bought this vehicle last week and I didn't notice that there was a gash in the wood grain of the steering wheel. I would like to get it replaced." The service man replied, "Um, this is not covered under the manufacturer warranty." I said, "May I please speak to Jay?" Jay was the customer service supervisor who gave me his card when I bought the truck and advised that if I ever needed anything to please let him know. It was time to take him up on his offer. Luckily, Jay was in the office and remembered me. He said, "What's going on Mr. Montanez?" I explained my situation and he said, "let me see what I can do." Notice, that Jay did not tell me what he could not do! This is very important in caring. People do not want to hear what you cannot do, they want to hear what you can do! When Jay came back, he had a receipt in hand to show me that he had written down the problem and had made note of it. He said, "Mr. Montanez we have a really good mechanic that has a lot of experience and can sand it down and smooth it out to be brand new." I looked at him through the corner of my eye and he knew that this is not what I was really looking for. At this point, Jay knew that it was time to play his best defense. Jay quickly said, if he cannot fix it, I will have someone in "Make Ready" give you a call." I complied and left the dealership. I must admit, when I left the dealership I said to myself, "Here we go, I've been down this road before! They said that they will call me and I will never receive a call." I was already preparing in my head what I was going to say once I returned to the dealership after no one had called me. To my surprise two days later, a man by the name of David called me and said, "Mr. Montanez I will be replacing your steering wheel for you but we are currently out of stock of that item. It usually takes two to three weeks for that stock to be replenished. I will give you a call once the steering wheel arrives and we will arrange a time to replace it. How does that sound?" I must say I said, "Whoa!" I was pleasantly surprised that someone actually followed through and did what they said they were going to do. By the way, this is sad that I was this excited about someone doing what they said they were going to do and took ownership. This is a real opportunity for businesses to leverage because it seems that ownership, integrity, and pride are things of the past. Anyway, I digress! To make a long story short, I got a brand new steering wheel, a car wash, and the interior vacuumed. Needless to say, I was very impressed. Jay and David saw the opportunity to play Defense and preserve the Toyota brand. They displayed a sense of ownership and took to heart the "Toyota Way". Sure, they could have played the role of the "Policy Police" (we'll talk about this later), but they were empowered to take care of the customer and do what is right. They knew that how they handled the situation would mean positive or negative energy towards their brand. They knew that the way they acted was a representation of the Toyota brand. This is very important for any customer facing employee to not only understand but to live. Furthermore, it is even more important that their leadership acknowledge and lead the way through their actions. In this case, I received what I wanted which was a new steering wheel. In all honesty, if they could have just sanded it down and made it right, I probably would have been ok with that. At the end of the day, it is not about giving customers what they want, or letting the customer take advantage, but more importantly, telling the customer what you can do! As you can see, my experience made me toot Toyota's diligence in dealing with my situation. Many people now know about my positive experience. How many people will buy a Toyota because of my experience? I have absolutely no idea. However, what I can tell you is that same promotion could have been negative towards the Toyota brand. So, what kind of promotion do you want for your business? Are your employees currently playing Offense and Defense?

CODE RED! CODE RED!

In order to care you must have a sense of urgency. The sense of urgency that I am referring to goes hand in hand with the A&A principle that was discussed in the "Lead" section. Nowadays, consumers have options and will pay more for service and convenience. For example, I made car rental reservations with a well known rental agency a month prior to my trip to Portland, Oregon for a very good corporate rate (4 days,$160, & for a full-size vehicle). I was elated. The day had finally come and I was excited to 1) see Portland & 2) rent my vehicle that I thought I received such a great price on. I even called the rental car agency that day to confirm my reservation and to see if there would be any issues with my arrival time of 11pm. I was assured by the representative that there would be no problem with the time that my flight arrived. I even joked with the representative and asked if a Bentley would be considered a full-size vehicle, he replied, "Um yeah at Buckingham Palace." Like I said, I was ready and happy. After a long 4-hour flight and a 2 hour change in time, I was met with a line at this rental agency comparable to American Idol auditions. Ok, it wasn't that long, but it was at least 12–15 people deep. I took a deep breath and told myself, "control what you can control." Being the observant eagle that I am, I noticed a sign at the far right of the counter that read, "Corporate Partners and Premier Members Line up here." I proceeded to go to the counter expecting to get more efficient service because that's what the sign said and I met the criteria. So I thought. Having been in the care industry for some time, I always dissect the interactions that employees have with the customers and the leadership presence. What I noticed was a lack of urgency as the attendant was having side bar conversations with the customer that she was helping while there stood 15 people waiting in line. I also noticed that there were only two representatives tasked to service the line. After twenty minutes of standing at the counter, the line not moving, and my presence not even being acknowledged, I looked over to my right and saw one of the rental agency's major competitors working more efficiently and effectively. As a matter of fact, both agencies had the same type of line when I first walked into the rental terminal and this other rental agency had already serviced their line of customers. So what was the difference? Was the other agency better? The other agency was staffed appropriately for a late night rush and they were working with a sense of urgency because they knew that the longer a customer waits, the poorer the customer experience.

After noticing that there was no one left in line, I made eye contact with the representative from the other car rental agency and decided to inquire about rental rates and availability. Thankfully, I was greeted with a welcoming tone and a smile. Clearly, the representative saw me waiting in line and was glad to take market share away from their competition. By the way, after about a two-minute discussion, I rented a brand new SUV from the other rental agency, paid $150 more for the rental, and was very satisfied. Needless to say, I was won over by a major competitor that leveraged my distaste at the time, was happy to help me, and acted with a sense of urgency. Code Red, Code Red, Care for you customers with the same sense of urgency as if it were you!

THE PRINCIPLE-PRINCIPLE!

Customers have the means to act on principle and the way they believe that things should be. I would often hear customers say, "It's not about the money, it's about the principle!" The days of customers being deterred by paying early termination fees for not fulfilling contracts are long gone. Customers believe in the Principle-Principle and you should too. Earlier we discussed A&A. Associating & Adapting is paramount when dealing with a situation where there is a cognition of principality.

If a company chooses to disregard the Principle-Principle that consumers have, it has to make sense. It cannot be a "dumb policy" and it has to be able to be rationally communicated for it to justifiably make sense to the consumer. Have you ever been challenged by a customer about a policy or procedure that your company had in place and had no idea how to combat it because you agreed with the customer, but, because it was the company's policy you just went along with it? Do not fret! You are not alone. I have had that feeling along with many others. Successful organizations utilize their customer facing employees to create policies and procedures that benefit the customer and the organization. After all, retaining customers is the key and sometimes the lost component in sustained growth. Customers will fire a company off of the Principle-Principle! Don't believe me? Take this experience that I had for example.

You can do almost everything from your smart phone nowadays via applications. One day I had downloaded an application to manage my Satellite TV account via self-serve, because this is more cost effective for companies and it is easier for me to not pick up the phone, be put on hold, get transferred from rep to rep, and fiddle with an automated system before getting a live person. So, after I downloaded the application, I noticed that there was a way to order Pay-Per View movies for $3.99. So I did. After I submitted my request, I received an error message that the order was not successful. I proceeded to turn to the channel that the movie was on and it was not active. Clearly, this application was not working as it should. I tried to order the movie a second time and I received the same error message. I again turned to the movie channel and the movie was still not on. I assumed that since I received the error message and the movie was not playing when I turned to the channel, that the transaction was unsuccessful. I gave up and said that I'll just go to the Red Box and I did. Later that month, I received a bill that showed two charges for the movie that I attempted to order but never received. Sure, two charges of $3.99 did not break my bank, however, I was overcome by the Principle-Principle. I felt it was unjust to pay for a service that I never received no matter what the cost. So, I called customer care and was greeted by a lackadaisical representative (I could tell by the tone in which she answered the phone). In my mind, I thought to myself, "here we go, this is going to be interesting." I went on to explain how I had downloaded the application, tried to order a movie via that application, received an error message, never watched the movie, and the fact that I was charged on my bill for a service that I never received. There was no empathy. I was placed on hold. When the representative returned, she explained that I was given a Pay-Per View credit for a Boxing match that I had ordered 10 months ago. I explained to the representative that I received that credit because there was a thunderstorm causing my satellite TV to go out and how I didn't get to watch it. She went on to say that it was the company's policy to only issue one credit per year per customer no matter what the circumstance. By the way, never quote company policy to a customer. Customers don't care what the company's policies are. I asked the representative if she were in my shoes would her response be acceptable? She replied, "Yes". At this point, I asked how much it would cost to cancel my service. She advised, "$60." I proceeded to do the math in my head, "I've paid $115 per month multiplied for the last 36 months (3yr customer), $4,140 and there is no understanding." "Ok, cancel my service." The representative replies, "Ok let me get you to one of our cancellation specialist." I'm thinking, "Wow they really don't value my business." Service cancelled. I will never choose that company again. Now, let's just think about how many people experienced that same service? Customer Wins and Company loses because of the Principle-Principle and a lack of caring! It was obvious that the representative was part of the policy police! There are too many options available to customers for a company to quote policy during circumstances where it is not applicable.

WHOOP WHOOP IT'S THE POLICY POLICE!

The Satellite TV representative is a prime example of the Policy Police. The Policy Police are protectors of the company policy. They have no diversity of thought and only do what the company says their policy or procedures are. There are never exceptions in their minds. It is either Black or White. There is no Gray! They have to stay in compliance all the time and there will be no deviation from the policy. Most probably, their leader leads from the compliance based approached rather than from the values based approach. This is frustrating not only from the customer perspective, but from that of the employee as well. Food for thought: Have you ever experienced the policy police at the work place or as a consumer? How did it make you feel? Did they show you that they cared?

The policy police protects policy even if it is a thoughtless policy. I feel this is an easy way out. Their leadership is not challenging them enough to empathize and find innovative ways to resolve issues; even if it has never been done before. When asked the question, "Why is that the policy/procedure?" and the only answer is, "Because that's the way it has always been done!" That is a formula for disaster. What if a competitor had that same policy but recognized it as "dumb" and not customer friendly, but the only difference is that they have the attitude that business must be flexible and change with the times/climate. Let's set a premise on the use of the term "dumb policy". I think we all agree that it is a matter of perspective on what one considers to be "dumb." I can think something is "dumb" but another can think the same exact thing is not. The case of a "dumb policy/procedure" refers to things that do not make matters simple and complicate situations unnecessarily. I am not inferring that there is no room for policy/procedures and there should not be any checks and balances. Of course there needs to be policies/procedures in place. Moreover, if that policy/ procedure is not making it easy for consumers to do business, is adding unnecessary steps, and is not optimizing the organizations efficiency and effectiveness, then it's "dumb!" Would you move your business (where you spend your hard earned cash) from a company that says No to a company that says Yes?

SAY NO TO NO

"No" is the worst word you can say along with "can't" and "won't." I can't do that. I won't be able to do that. Customers want to know what you can do. How about this! Say, "Yes, I can definitely look into that for you" or "Let's see what can be done" or "What we can do for you is..." In my experience, businesses can do whatever it is that they want to do. Pay particular attention to the word "want." It is a matter of what the employee and the business want to do. How do I know this? Because I have led the frontline and anything can be done if there is a will. It may not be done right away and it may take some thinking (work) but anything can be done. I've done it! Nothing illustrates this more than the case of the "accidental airline reservation."

My best friend and I planned to take a trip and I was the person appointed to make the airline reservations. I proceeded to go online and purchase two tickets on the same flight. I immediately received the confirmation email and noticed that I had made a boo-boo. I inadvertently did not put my best friend's name as the second passenger; it was showing my name on both tickets. Without delay I called the airline customer service line and proceeded to explain my honest mistake. I was thinking to myself, "All I did was accidentally put my name on both tickets on the same flight, the airline representative would understand, change the name to the correct name, and I would go on with my night." This was not the case. The customer service representative told me no they could not do that even though the tickets were just purchased less than five minutes ago. So I asked, "What could be done?" She put me on hold and when she came back to the line she advised that her supervisor said that it could not be done. The resolution would be for my best friend and I to drive to the airport (1 hour away) and show our identification at the ticket counter to change the name. This is clearly not what I wanted to hear. However, I remained calm and proceeded to politely ask to speak with her supervisor. After holding for 10 minutes, the supervisor came on the line and said, "Unfortunately, we can't change the name on the ticket!" I explained that I had just clicked "purchase" less than five minutes of calling the airline and noticed my honest error right away. I asked, "Is there any way we can just change the name as I made an honest mistake?" She replied, "No." I'm thinking to myself WOW! So, I asked her a provocative question. I said, "Ms. Supervisor, why in my right mind would I purchase two tickets, for the same flight, with the same name? If you were in my shoes, made an honest mistake, and needed help, how would you feel if someone gave you the same answer that you gave me?" After about ten seconds of silence on the phone she said, "Mr. Montanez let me put you on hold for a second." She came back to the line and advised that the name had been changed and this is not something that is usually done but given the circumstances an exception was made. I'm thinking to myself, "Couldn't we have gotten this done an hour earlier?"

The moral of the story is that businesses need to empower (refer to DEED of Trust) their employees, especially those that are customer facing, to say no to no. Just because historically the answer has been no, it does not mean the answer has to be "no" all the time. Businesses must take every customer for what he or she is; unique individuals. Unique individuals, will at some point have unique concerns/requests, which will call for unique resolutions. The organization that empowers their employees to think quickly and innovatively will have a greater competitive advantage.

SERVICED VS. PROCESSED

How does it feel when you go into your local Department of Motor Vehicles (DMV)? How can I help you, take this number, when your number is called go to the counter, agent will take care of you, you're now on your way. I don't know about you, but it feels like I'm just a number and I do not like the way that feels. This feeling is not just limited to the DMV but to any place where one feels as if he is being placed on a conveyer belt. It is not even about having a logistical process in place to serve a customer, but more about the interpersonal part. It is imperative to have a smile, a welcoming tone, and a confident posture when serving a customer. When I use the term "customer", I am referring to both internal as well as external customers. In a sales environment, I would say processing and clerking go hand in hand. Let me give you an example: Customer walks in and asks for something, you give a monotone welcome, you get that something, ask will this be it?, customer says yes, you ring it up, customer pays and is on his/her way. The customer was processed.

Being serviced is the same as being educated. When you educate, you're adding value. So, servicing a customer is adding value. Nowadays, people have busy lives and there is an opportunity to proactively service customers and add value. Customers depend on their service providers to be the subject matter experts. So what else do customers want? Although I stated earlier that every customer is unique, there are some commonalities that all customers share. **CARE** is the way:

C–Consistency

A–Acknowledgement

R–Resolve

E–Efficiency

CONSISTENCY: All consumers want a consistent experience. No one likes surprises. How do you feel, when you open up an invoice and it is different from what you were told or agreed to? If you say that you are going to do something, make sure you do it. If you say something will work this way, make sure that it works this way. If you give an answer to a customer's question, make sure that they will get the same answer if they asked someone else in your organization. How many times have you been given an answer by one person and then ask the same question to another person and receive a different answer? When you are brushed off and given any answer just to get rid of you, is care exhibited? Consistency is key. Consistency breeds loyalty. Think about it. Did you exhibit more loyalty to a significant other who consistently showed you love, support, and care than one who didn't? The same works in business. Be consistent!

ACKNOWLEDGEMENT: How did it make you feel when you walked into a store and were not acknowledged as a patron? How about when you walked over to the airline counter and were not greeted with the best of attitudes or perhaps looked over completely? Or, how about when you put much time and energy into your appearance or a meal, or a gift for a significant other and he/she did not acknowledge your effort? People like to feel acknowledged. When you are about to spend your hard earned cash somewhere and you are not acknowledged, that does not demonstrate care. An acknowledgement can be as easy as creating good eye contact, a smile, or just simply saying a genuine hello. There is always an opportunity to acknowledge a customer, supplier, employee, or a stranger. Taking the time to address a person by his/her name is a key ingredient in acknowledgement and caring. Have you ever seen someone needing help from another person and then look down on them like they are beneath them? But, they needed that person to help them or resolve an issue for them. When was the last time that you were at the checkout line and acknowledged the attendant by using his/her first name? How about when you were out to dinner, did you acknowledge your server by using his/her first name? Try it! You might make someone's day by acknowledging them.

RESOLVE: There are two ways for us to look at resolve; from a customer standpoint and a service provider standpoint. From a customer standpoint, nothing else shows how much you care than resolving an issue or concern the first time. The key is for one to show that he cares enough to take ownership and have a sense of urgency as if it were his problem. It is not the talk about providing excellent service that matters but the action. I once heard a saying, "Your actions are so loud that I cannot hear what you are saying!" This holds true when we talk about resolve. In an ideal world, the customer should not have to speak to someone more than once to resolve a situation. Organizations must seek first time resolutions in an efficient manner.

An organization must show resolve when it comes to caring for its customers. When I speak about customers, I'm referring to internal and external customers. It takes great resolve to show that you care. Employees and customers may be disgruntled at some point and I agree that you cannot always make everyone happy. However, it takes great resolve not to give up on an employee or a customer. I am a firm believer that there is good in everyone, some may be more difficult to get through to than others, but look for the good and have resolve. It is extremely costly to be constantly looking for employees and customers after investing heavily in them to bring them on. There is always a reason why someone acts or feels a certain way. Find out why and resolve it!

EFFICIENCY: Time is money. Time is valuable. Time flies. I want things done when I want them done. Many people share these sentiments. Nowadays, patience is very limited because there are so many choices. If one place takes too long then we just go somewhere else. Remember my car rental experience? It is for this reason that efficiency is so important. It all boils down to acting with a sense of urgency. Light a fire to get the most done while maximizing your effectiveness. It is impossible to show that you care if you do not show that you are demonstrating that you are as efficient as possible. By acknowledging that a customer's time is valuable and operating in this manner shows that you are attempting to be as efficient as possible. Have you ever been to a doctor's office and waited for thirty minutes or more past your scheduled appointment time? Did you feel that your time was valued?

Putting it all together, it is obvious that all the components of CARE are essential to truly care. One cannot be consistent, be acknowledging, resolve the issue, and lack efficiency. Similarly, if one resolves the issue the first time, is consistent, is efficient but has a poor attitude in the acknowledgement department, care is still not exhibited. In other words, put it all together and CARE to truly show that you care.

WHOA!

Why does Chic-Fil-A have a line wrapped around the building every time I go through the drive through and I wait? Is the chicken really that good? Well, maybe, but I can tell you that every time I speak to a drive through attendant over the intercom and interact with them face to face, I'm greeted with a welcoming tone. As a matter of fact, I distinctly remember the time one attendant said with a bright smile, "Thank you so much for your business and we'll see you tomorrow!" I don't remember if I went back the next day, however, I sure did think of it. Why does USAA Insurance and Banking always dominate Net Promoter Score (NPS) across industries? How does Southwest dominate the Airlines when it comes to customer satisfaction in an industry not known for its customer friendly approach? What makes people wait in an Apple store for service when it's packed? Why do you consistently do business with those that you have a choice to do business with? It's the Whoa factor!

Whoa is what your customers should be saying every time they come into contact with someone from your organization. They should be out of breath because you serviced them and took so much care of them. Furthermore, they should release a big fat Whoa from a rooftop letting all know that they have been cared for! Customers should be in awe that every time they do business with your organization, irrespective of who is assisting them, they receive the same whoa experience. There is great opportunity here because unfortunately, as employees and consumers, that whoa experience doesn't happen consistently enough. It is the difference between servicing versus processing and CARE-ing. The example of the Chic-Fil-A attendant is a situation where a customer chooses to go through a process (the drive-through) but the culture of the organization demands that the customer be serviced. The difference is that when you service a customer/client you are adding value and exceeding expectations. When you process a customer, you are meeting the minimum expectation. Consequently, if you only meet the minimum expectation, a difference is not made, resulting in a customer just being satisfied. I previously mentioned how customer satisfaction is worthless and the difference between servicing and processing a customer. In what ways do you make your internal and external customers say "Whoa?" Here's a golden nugget. If you want your frontline employees to deliver a whoa experience all the time, ensure that their leadership delivers a whoa experience all the time. In other words, show them how to do it through your actions in taking care of them as their leader.

CARE-ING IS THE BEST SELLING

Often times, people get so consumed in selling that they forget about caring. Some people have an attitude that if it is not making them money then it is not worth their time. This is a poor attitude to have because caring leads to trust, which leads to relationships, which leads to referrals, which leads to sustainable sales. People do business with others who care about that what they feel is important. For example, personally, I feel follow-up and keeping one's word is vital. If someone does not care enough to follow-up or keep their word, I do not do business with them. When I was an account executive, my customers cared about me answering the phone when they called, resolving any issues/concerns within a timely manner, and doing what I said I was going to do. So, I cared to do just that through my actions. When the phone rang, I picked it up, when something needed a resolution, I resolved it, and when I said something was going to happen, it happened. This had a direct correlation to the sales that I received from these companies when there was business to be earned and referrals to be made. Unfortunately, this was not the case across the board. Some of my colleagues, (who were older and more tenured) for whatever reason, did not get this very elementary concept.

I guess some people just don't want to put the work in. I mean, I don't mind, it was more opportunity for me. In this competitive environment, if you do not care, someone else will. Plenty of people get it and will uncover additional needs and turn them into sales with your "problem customer."

Nothing tells the story better than when one of my colleagues asked me if I can take over the account of one of his "problem customers" because, as he described it, it was "technically in my territory" (we were assigned territories based on zip codes). Without hesitation, I said, "sure." So, I set up an appointment that week, allowed the customer to vent about my colleague, uncovered what the actual issue was, resolved the issue within a day, and uncovered a big deal that was right under his nose if he would have just cared about what the customer cared about! Now, it's all mine!

Pay attention to what your customers or potential customers care about with the same vigor that you care or should care about someone that you absolutely love; you will succeed!

EPILOGUE

Leadership, Sales, and Care are fundamental concepts that need attention more than ever in today's business environment. Whether you are involved in it for profit, non-profit, in the government space, or are a business owner, one thing is certain. If you don't have the ability to influence behavior, sell yourself, and care for the customers (both internal and external) that you have, you will not be maximizing your potential. The key is having leaders that want to lead at every level of the organization and to eventually develop them into Catapult Leaders that simplify the business thereby making it easy to do business. Lead, Sell, Care as easy as 1,2,3...is not easy and is a constant work in progress. Remember, Ability (Skill), Awareness, and Will (Commitment) must exist to realize break-through results. Are you and your organization focusing enough resources (time, money, and energy) on the fundamentals of Leading, Selling, & Caring? If not, don't wait, the time is now! Call me. ☺

QUOTES THAT MAKE YOU GO HMMMMM...

Please take the time out to enjoy quotes that I have retained along the way that have helped me to reflect, provoke thought, and take action.

"I don't know the key to success, but the key to failure is trying to please everybody." – Bill Cosby

"Opportunities are never lost. The other fellow takes those you miss."

"We must accept finite disappointment, but never lose infinite hope."
– Martin Luther King, Jr.

Train up a child in the way he should go: and when he is old, he will not depart from it. – Proverbs 22:6

"Seize the day, put no trust in the morrow." – Horace (65 B. C. - 8 B.C.)

"Every man has his own destiny: the only imperative is to follow it, to accept it, no matter where it leads him."

"Too many people are ready to carry the stool when the piano needs to be moved." – Anonymous

If a house be divided against itself, that house cannot stand. – Mark 3:25

If God be for us, who can be against us? – Hebrews 8:31

"*Effort and courage are not enough without purpose and direction.*"
– John F. Kennedy

"*Life consists not in holding good cards but in playing those you hold well.*"
– Josh Billings

He that is not with me is against me. – Luke 11:23

"*Nothing tells more about the character of a man than the things he makes fun of.*" – Johanne Goethe

"*You must do the things you think you cannot do.*" – Eleanor [Anna] Roosevelt

Ask, and it shall be given you; Seek, and ye shall find; Knock, and it shall be opened unto you. – Matthew 7:7

"*The very essence of Leadership is that you have to have a vision.*"
– Theodore Hesburgh

"*Leadership is the capacity to translate vision into reality.*" – Walter Winchell

"Be at peace with yourself first and then you will be able to bring peace to others." – Thomas A. Kempis

They that sow in tears shall reap joy. – Psalms 126:5

"Courage, the footstool of the Virtues, upon which they stand."
– Robert Louis [Balfour] Stevenson

"Pick battles big enough to matter, small enough to win." – Jonathan Kozol

"Success is getting what you want. Happiness is liking what you get."

As a man thinks in his heart, so is he. – Proverbs 23:7

The truth shall set you free. – John 8:32

"Despair is the price one pays for setting oneself an impossible aim."
– Graham Greene

"We can do anything we want to if we stick to it long enough." – Helen Keller

For whoever keeps the whole law and yet stumbles at just one point is guilty of breaking all of it. – James 2:9-11

"Advice is like snow; the softer it falls, the longer it dwells upon, and the deeper it sinks into the mind." – Samuel Coleridge

Who of you by worrying can add a single hour to his life or single cubit to his height? – Matthew 6:26-28

Be swift to hear, slow to speak, slow to wrath. – James 1:19

Evil communications corrupt good manners. – 1 Corinthians 15:33

When I was a child, I spoke, understood and thought as a child; but when I became a man, I put away childish things. – 1 Corinthians 13:11

The race is not (always) to the swift, nor the battle to the strong. – Ecclesiastes 9:11

And let us not be weary in well doing: for in due season we shall reap, if we faint not. – Galatians 6:9

"Through perseverance many people win success out of what seemed destined to be certain failure." – Benjamin Disraeli

"Small deeds done are better than great deeds planned." – Peter Marshall

"Do one thing at a time, and do that one thing as if your life depended on it." – Eugene Grace

"It is only with the heart that one can see rightly; what is essential is invisible to the eye." – Antoine de Saint-Exupery

"Teaching kids to count is fine, but teaching them what counts is best."
– Bob Talbert

Do unto others as you would have others do unto you. – Matthew 7:120

"Bad habits are like a comfortable bed, easy to get into, but hard to get out of." – Anonymous

Great men are not always wise. – Job 32:9

"It is not length of life, but depth of life." – Ralph Waldo Emerson

"Sour, sweet, bitter, pungent, all must be tasted." – Chinese Proverb

"Now is no time to think of what you do not have. Think of what you can do with what there is." – Ernest Hemingway

"Sometimes you earn more by doing the jobs that pay nothing."
– Todd Ruthman

"All the knowledge I possess everyone else can acquire, but my heart is still my own." – Johann Wolfgang

What profit is it to a man if he gains the whole world, & lose his own soul? Or what will a man give in exchange for his soul? – Matthew 16:26

We walk by faith, not by sight. – 2 Corinthians 5:7

"He is able who thinks he is able." – Buddha

"The strongest principle of growth lies in the human choice." – George Eliot

"The way I see it, if you want the rainbow, you gotta put up with the rain."
– Dolly Parton

"Success follows doing what you want to do. There is no other way to be successful." – Malcolm Forbes

"Hope is the denial of reality." – Anonymous

Stone is heavy and sand a burden, but provocation by a fool is heavier than both. – Proverbs 27:3

If your life is to flash before your eyes some day, make sure that it's worth watching. – Unknown

"In three words I can sum up everything I've learned about life: it goes on."
– Robert [Lee] Frost

"Opportunities multiply as they are seized." – Sun Tzu

Judge not according to the appearance. – John 7:24

It is more blessed to give than to receive. – Acts 20:35

"*A man is but a product of his thoughts; what he thinks, that he becomes.*"
– *Mohandas Karamchand Gandhi*

"*The ambitious climbs up high and perilous stairs, and never cares how to come down.*" – *Thomas Adams*

"*Playing without the fundamentals is like eating without a knife and a fork. You make a mess.*" – *Dick Williams*

"*What you do speaks so loudly that I cannot hear what you say.*"
– *Ralph Waldo Emerson*

"*Action may not always bring happiness; but there is no happiness without action.*" – *Benjamin Disraeli*

"*We all came on different ships, but we are in the same boat now.*"
– *Martin Luther King, Jr*

"*Stagnant water loses its purity & in cold weather becomes frozen: even so does inaction sap the vigors of the mind.*" – *Leonardo da Vinci*

"*Things turn out best for those that make the best of the way things turn out.*"
– *Art Linkletter*

"Be true to your work, your word, and your friend." – *Henry David Thoreau*

"Patience and perseverance have a magical effect before which difficulties disappear and obstacles vanish." – *John Quincy Adams*

"Expect people to be better than they are, it helps them to become better." – *Merry Browne*

"Just because your voice reaches halfway around the world doesn't mean you're wiser than when it reached the end of the bar." – *Edward Murrow*

"He that is good for making excuses is seldom good for anything else." – *Ben Franklin*

"True courage is not the absence of fear; rather it is the taking of action in spite of the fear." – *Anonymous*

"Plenty of people miss their share of happiness. Not because they never find it, but because they didn't stop to enjoy it." – *William Feather*

"Someone is sitting in the shade today because someone planted a tree a long time ago." – *Warren Buffet*

"It isn't what you have, or who you are that makes you happy or unhappy. It is what you think about." – *Dale Carnegie*

"There is only one thing more painful than learning from experience and that is not learning from experience." – Archibald McLeish

"The foolish person seeks happiness in the distance, the wise person grows it under his feet." – James Oppenheim

"There is no limit to what can be accomplished if it doesn't matter who gets the credit." – Emerson

"When we long for life without difficulties, remind us that oaks grow strong in contrary winds." – Peter Marshall

"Do the right thing. It will gratify some people and astonish the rest." – Mark Twain

"I find that the harder I work, the more luck I seem to have." – Thomas Jefferson

"I hear and I forget. I see and I remember. I do and I understand." – Confucius

"Change does not necessarily assure progress, but progress implacably requires change." – Henry Steele Commager

"When the effective leader is finished with his work, the people say it happened naturally." – Lao Tse

"Winning is habit. Unfortunately, so is losing." – Vince Lombardi

"It is better to be defeated on principle than to win on lies." – Arthur Caldwell

"Those who dare to fail miserably can achieve greatly." – Robert F. Kennedy

"If you're not learning while you're earning, you're cheating yourself out of the better portion of your compensation." – Napoleon Hill

"No man was ever endowed with a right without being at the same time saddled with a responsibility." – Gerald W. Johnson

"Character is made by many acts, but can be lost with a single one" – Anonymous

"You can't get much done in life if you only work on the days when you feel good." – Jerry West

"Kind words can be short and easy to speak, but their echoes are truly endless." – Mother Teresa

"Expecting the world to be fair because you're a good person is like expecting a bull not to attack because you're vegetarian." – D Wholey

"Remember not only to say the right thing in the right place, but leave unsaid the wrong thing at the tempting moment." – Ben Franklin

"Trouble is only opportunity in work clothes." – *Henry J. Kaiser*

"Opportunity is missed by most people because it is dressed in overalls and looks like work." – *Thomas Edison*

"A Scholar who cherishes the love of comfort is not fit to be deemed a scholar." – *Lao-Tzu*

"Some men see things as they are and say why? I dream things that never were and say 'Why not?" – *Robert Kennedy*

"Chaotic action is preferable to orderly inaction." – *Will Rogers*

"It is better to train 10 people, than to do the work of ten people. But it is harder." – *Moody*

REFERENCES

Reichheld, F. (2006) *The Ultimate Question: Driving Good Profits and True Growth*. Boston, MA. Harvard Business School Publishing.

Maxwell, J. C.(2005) *The 360degree Leader: Developing your Influence from Anywhere in the Organization*. Nashville, TN. Nelson Business.

Cottrell, D. (2002) *Monday Morning Leadership: 8 Mentoring Sessions You Can't Afford to Miss*. Dallas, TX. CornerStone Leadership Institute.